From Junkie to Jerusalen
tantly, it's a captivating st
life of Larry Huch, one (
an authentic Christian le;
has been an outspoken friend to, and champion for, the nation and
people of Israel.

—MIKE HUCKABEE
FORMER GOVERNOR OF ARKANSAS,
APPOINTED US AMBASSADOR TO ISRAEL

Pastor Larry Huch's "journey of destiny" should be part of everyone's journey—a return to Jerusalem and its history, values, and divine message. Take that journey with Pastor Huch and rediscover the ancient truths that are as compelling today as they were thousands of years ago.

—DAVID M. FRIEDMAN
FORMER US AMBASSADOR TO ISRAEL

Pastor Larry Huch, perhaps the greatest master of Torah teaching in the Christian world, brings us the inspiring real-life story of his courageous odyssey told with searing honesty and unshakeable conviction. Living his journey changed the author; reading it will change the reader.

—RABBI DANIEL LAPIN
AMERICAN ALLIANCE OF JEWS AND CHRISTIANS

Mazel Tov to Pastor Larry on the release of his new book! Pastor Larry and Tiz, along with New Beginnings Church and Larry Huch Ministries, are guided by a unique and profound calling. Their dedication, courage, and commitment set an inspiring example for others, standing firm in support of the people and land of Israel. Pastor Larry's work on highlighting the Jewish roots of faith has been transformative, fostering understanding and connection between Jews and Christians and helping to break down walls that have existed for centuries.

For over eleven years, Pastor Larry and I have worked side by side on the board of the Israel Allies Foundation, cooperating with other leaders to influence governments around the world to support Israel politically, tangibly, and with concrete results. Pastor Larry has been an unwavering advocate, using his voice and energy to stand up for Israel on the global stage. It is truly an honor to call him a dear friend and ally, and I look forward to continuing our shared work to make a lasting impact together.

—JOSH REINSTEIN
PRESIDENT, ISRAEL ALLIES FOUNDATION; DIRECTOR, KNESSET
CHRISTIAN ALLIES CAUCUS

Pastor Larry is a man of God, distinguished by a remarkable calling and saved by Christ in a supernatural way. His testimony is powerful and impactful, and he stands among the most anointed preachers of all time, possessing deep theological insight and an unwavering commitment to defending the cause of Israel. Pastor Larry's ministry has profoundly influenced my life through the power of the revealed Word, and he has been mightily used to ignite the work of the Holy Spirit across Brazil and the entire world. I am honored to call him a friend, and the people of Brazil are deeply grateful for his dedication, love, care, prayers, and the strong bond he shares with our nation.

—APOSTLE ESTEVAM HERNANDES
FOUNDER, REBORN IN CHRIST CHURCH;
LEADER, THE MARCH FOR JESUS BRAZIL

Pastor Larry Huch is a visionary leader and a renowned authority on the Old Testament and Israel. His generous spirit has touched nations across the globe, including our beloved Brazil. I am truly honored to call him my friend.

—EDUARDO BORTOLOSSI
SENIOR PASTOR, IGREJA FAMÍLIA
SÃU PAULO, BRAZIL

We have had the privilege to know and be in relationship with Pastors Larry and Tiz for thirty wonderful years. Since we first met in 1994 on their first trip to Zimbabwe, we have had the utmost love and respect for them. Pastor Larry's testimony is equal to Paul's road to Damascus experience. The total transformation and effects of the Holy Spirit on Pastor Larry are as evident today as on that first engagement. I have no doubt that his motivation for being in the ministry is his incredible gratitude for the life-changing deliverance he received from our mighty God.

Pastor Larry preaches the Word of God with such boldness and conviction to both Jew and Gentile. He and Pastor Tiz have such a heart to be an extension of God's provision for the vulnerable in society. Here in Zimbabwe, we have seen firsthand their love and commitment in faithfully and continuously bringing relief to the suffering. Thank you and God bless you, or as we would say in the Shona language, *Ndatenda, uye Mwari vakuropafadzei!*

—DESMOND AND GLENDA NAUDE
CHIREDZI, ZIMBABWE

Since the seventh of October we were called to duty in the Israel Defense Force (IDF) Military Reserve. Shortly after the beginning of the war, we received the military ambulance Pastors Larry and Tiz sent to us. This ambulance was a home for our soldiers, an emergency room for the wounded, and in some cases a place to pay the last respects to the deceased. We also had the honor of receiving released hostages in the vehicle they sent.

It is so meaningful, not only for the vehicle itself, but for the touching gesture, to feel that a community so far away in Texas cares enough to go out of their way for our well-being. Pastors Larry and Tiz Huch, New Beginnings Church, and Larry Huch Ministries, thank you very much. We are very touched.

—GUY SEGALOVITCH
BATTALION COMMANDER, IDF MILITARY RESERVE

We want to express our deepest gratitude once again to Pastors Larry and Tiz Huch, New Beginnings Church, and Larry Huch Ministries for their generous gifts to American Friends of Magen David Adom (AFMDA) in support of Magen David Adom's emergency relief efforts in Israel. Their generous donations in purchasing ambulances and humanitarian aid have had great impact on Magen David Adom, as well as on the health and safety of the Israeli people.

—RICHARD D. ZELIN
DIRECTOR OF STRATEGIC PHILANTHROPY, MIDWEST REGION,
AMERICAN FRIENDS OF MAGEN DAVID ADOM
ISRAEL

I have been privileged to know Pastor Larry for the past eight years. He is a true friend of the Jewish people and the State of Israel, and most importantly, has the unique ability to build bridges between Christians and Jews, to help them learn about each other, love each other, and partner to fulfill Bible prophecy.

I have partnered with Pastor Larry on different projects for the benefit of the people of Israel, but I have three main memories that will remain with me for the rest of my life.

When the war broke out between Ukraine and Russia, and Israel was flooded with requests by Jews who wanted to return home, we immediately called Pastor Larry to ask for his help in rescuing our people. He launched an emergency campaign, utilizing every platform possible—TV, social media, etc.—to rescue these beleaguered Jews and bring them back to their ancestral homeland. Thousands of Russian and Ukrainian Jews owe their lives to Pastor Larry. Today they are living in the Jewish homeland, giving their children a Jewish education, and raising them in a Jewish environment.

Among the thousands of Jews he helped rescue were many Holocaust survivors. As the grandson of a Holocaust survivor, I cannot forget how Pastor Larry came to Ben Gurion airport to welcome a plane full of new immigrants from Ukraine, among them a ninety-two-year-old Holocaust survivor. Pastor Larry boarded the plane, took her hand, and escorted her off the plane. He gave her a hug and told her that the Christian people support her and that she is safe now.

Pastor Larry later asked to accompany a delegation of Christian leaders to Poland on Holocaust Remembrance Day and to march, together with tens of thousands of Jews, in the March of the Living from Auschwitz to Birkenau and declare: "Never Again." I will never forget Pastor Larry linking arms with former Chief Rabbi of Israel, Rabbi Israel Meir Lau, himself a Holocaust survivor. This image for me is a testament to the fact that we are living in an era of new relationships between Christians and Jews. Rabbi Lau and Pastor Larry have built a special, warm, and lasting friendship.

Pastor Larry is a man of action. On October 7, immediately after hearing the news of the massacre, he called our world chairman and me and asked how he could help. He spoke with his congregation and wherever else he could about the importance of supporting Israel in time of war. Through Keren Hayesod, Pastor Larry provided assistance to victims of terror, helped evacuate new immigrants from areas of danger, distributed food to needy Holocaust survivors, and more. In cooperation with NBC, he donated a military ambulance after many ambulances were destroyed on October 7.

That same military ambulance was later used to bring hostage Doron Asher, along with her two small daughters, home from the Egyptian border after they were kidnapped on October 7. Today

Doron and her daughters are healing and rebuilding their lives. For me, Pastor Larry is a role model of Christian Zionist leadership, a person of wisdom, love for the Jewish people, and support for Israel and a visionary who knows how to foster love and understanding between Jews and Christians.

—Shmulik Fried
Director, Friends of Israel
at Keren Hayesod–United Israel Appeal

Pastor Larry Huch is one of the most significant Christian religious leaders in the world. Through his life's story and personal journey, overcoming some of the greatest challenges to reach such a high position of public leadership, he serves as a source of inspiration. Especially noteworthy is his steadfast commitment to the principles of strengthening the State of Israel, strengthening the United States, and reinforcing the connection between them. Pastor Larry Huch serves as one of the key links in connecting global justice and is a great inspiration to his community and to many others.

—Yossi Dagan
Governor of Samaria

Larry Huch has established himself as one of the passionate advocates for Israel both in the United States and internationally. Through his ministry and diplomatic efforts, he has fearlessly championed Israel and the Jewish people in meetings with world leaders, including at the United Nations and the US Congress. Our shared visit to Auschwitz-Birkenau in Poland—where we witnessed the atrocities of the Holocaust—deepened his already profound commitment to fighting antisemitism and supporting Israel and the Jewish people.

—Rabbi Israel Meir Lau
Holocaust Survivor of Buchenwald Concentration Camp

FROM JUNKIE TO JERUSALEM

LARRY HUCH

CHARISMA
HOUSE

occur after publication. Further, the publisher and author do not have any control over and do not assume any responsibility for third-party websites or their content.

For more resources like this, visit MyCharismaShop.com and the author's website at larryhuchministries.com.

Cataloging-in-Publication Data is on file with the Library of Congress.
International Standard Book Number: 978-1-63641-450-8
E-book ISBN: 978-1-63641-451-5

1 2024
Printed in the United States of America

Most Charisma Media products are available at special quantity discounts for bulk purchase for sales promotions, premiums, fund-raising, and educational needs. For details, call us at (407) 333-0600 or visit our website at charismamedia.com.

The author has made every effort to provide accurate accounts of events, but he acknowledges that others may have different recollections of these events.

Some names and identifying details have been changed to protect the privacy of those individuals.

I dedicate this book to Tiz, my wife, love of my life, best friend and bashert—my soulmate. Nearly fifty years ago she walked into my life and captivated my attention, my heart, and my soul and has continued to every moment since! God truly brought us together for this incredible journey of life which we do completely together, in sync and in joy. She brings out the best in me and in everyone whose life she touches. She is the glue that keeps our family and our life together and on track. I would not be who I am or where I am today if it wasn't for her love, godliness, faith, support, courage, positive attitude, and strength. Through the best of times and the most challenging times, she is my rock. I love, appreciate, and thank God for her more and more every day!

I also dedicate this book to my incredible family. Our kids and their spouses—Anna and Brandin, Luke and Jen, and Katie, and our sugars (grandkids), Asher, Judah, Aviva, and Lion—are all the light of my life. Out of all the accomplishments of our lives, I am most proud of our family. They each love, honor, and are dedicated to God, our family, and God's people. Through our entire life's journey, they have made the most of all the changes, circumstances, and challenges and carved out their own identities, callings, and destinies. Each one knows and lives out that we are blessed to be a blessing. And they are the most fun, intriguing, and enjoyable people I know!

I know that our best is yet to come!

CONTENTS

FOREWORD

I WILL NEVER FORGET when, together with my colleague Shmulik Fried, I met Pastors Larry and Tiz Huch for the very first time and got to know New Beginnings Church and Larry Huch Ministries. It was some six years ago, and I recall this meeting so vividly and the impact it had on me in which I began to witness and understand the genuine and sincere love the people of Israel are blessed to have from our Christians friends of Israel.

Our partnership began when Pastor Larry started to support Aliyah, immigration of Jews to Israel, and take an active role in the fulfillment of Bible prophecy. Thanks to Pastors Larry and Tiz and New Beginnings Church, tens of thousands of Jews from all over the world were able to fulfill their dreams and destiny, immigrate to Israel, and raise their families in the land of their ancestors and the homeland of the Jewish people.

In addition, Pastor Larry and New Beginnings Church also helped Holocaust survivors, the elderly, and children suffering from post-trauma from the South of Israel, as a result of constant missile attacks they endured since early childhood.

I know that Pastors Larry and Tiz believe with all their

hearts that their lives have been blessed and the many challenges they and their families have struggled to overcome have been divinely impacted because of all they do for Israel and the Jewish people, as it says in Genesis 12:3: "I will bless those who bless you."

Friendship is measured not only in good times but mainly in difficult situations. With the outbreak of the war on October 7, Pastor Larry was one of the first calls I received, and he immediately asked, "Sam, I am now going to pray with my congregation. What do you need, how can we help?" Pastor Larry immediately began raising critically needed funds to help the affected families of terror, to evacuate new immigrants from danger areas, and to purchase mobile bomb shelters, ambulances, and much more.

I think back with great fondness to one of my visits to Dallas, when I spoke at New Beginnings Church at a Sunday service with my longtime friend, Israeli Minister of Strategic Affairs Ron Dermer, also former Israeli ambassador to the United States. Following the service, we attended a Dallas Cowboys football game with Pastor Larry. At some point during the game, Minister Dermer stepped aside to take a phone call from Israel and then returned and handed his cell phone to Pastor Larry and surprised him with a brief conversation with Israeli Prime Minister Benjamin (Bibi) Netanyahu, who thanked Pastor Larry for being such a staunch friend and supporter of Keren Hayesod and Israel.

I feel that on a personal level I have earned a friend and family member for life. I know that Keren Hayesod has gained a true partner and a true friend.

—SAM GRUNDWERG
WORLD CHAIRMAN OF KEREN HAYESOD
(UNITED ISRAEL APPEAL)

A PLEA FOR HAPPINESS

EVERYONE WENT INTO town, and I was alone at the ranch house. "Now's my chance," I thought. "This time, I'm going to push the limit and really get high."

My drug-smuggling friends and partners were worried about me. Sure, we were all users, but I had taken drugs to a whole new level, and my body and mind showed the effects. Thin and drawn, I weighed a mere 140 pounds, with needle scars dotting my tattooed arms. My overgrown Fu Manchu moustache and my long, wavy hair hanging halfway down my back accentuated the dark circles around my eyes, which were glazed and sunken into my hardened face. Ragged jeans and whatever loose-fitting wrinkled shirt I could toss on had become my usual attire. No one would have guessed that I was once a lean, mean 212-pound college football player, Golden Gloves boxer, and competitive weight lifter who took third place in the nation in my class.

But that was then. Now I was slowly killing myself and didn't know it—or maybe I did. I snorted coke, smoked weed, and drank all day long. That was pretty much my existence. I lived to get high. But all the snorting, smoking, and drinking on this day hadn't been enough. I needed more, so I decided to mainline the cocaine by shooting it straight into my veins. To ensure getting extra high, I doubled my normal dose. But because my veins had collapsed from all the shooting up, the needle missed the vein.

Unaware of what had happened, I thought, "Wow, I didn't feel a thing." So I doubled the dose again, inserted the needle, and missed the vein again, still without realizing it.

Feeling nothing but frustration, I did something only a foolish addict would do: I doubled the dose a third time. This time I hit the vein, sending a lethal dose of pure cocaine straight into my bloodstream. Almost instantly, my heart seemed to explode in rapid, violent palpitations that constricted my chest and caused labored breathing, trembling, and profuse sweating. As my body collapsed to the floor, I cried, "I'm dying! I'm dying!"

Then something strange happened—something surreal. In those split seconds of hovering between life and death, time stood still, and I became acutely aware of a bigger picture. I was aware enough to speak to my Creator, whoever that was. "God," I pleaded, "don't let me die until I find out what happiness is."

I'm the first to admit that a plea for happiness is a strange request from a dying man, but I had no real religious or Bible background as reference points. The little I knew about God came from my precious Aunt Helen and the old Catholic church that stood like a fortress on my neighborhood street corner. Somehow, God was supposed to be in there, surrounded by statues and religious artifacts. The priest was called *father*, but wrapping my mind around that idea was hard because of how my own dad had treated me.

No, my cry that day wasn't for salvation. "Just let me live

to find happiness" was my only request. I'd had very little happiness at home and no happy times with my dad—none. My growing up was brutal, abusive, and violent. In my desperate search for meaning and happiness, I tried an assortment of pathways: playing sports (which I was pretty good at), embracing an immoral lifestyle, making loads of money selling drugs, and, finally, using the hardest drugs in search of the ultimate high. All of these left a gaping void in my soul.

So I begged again, "God, please don't let me die until I find what happiness is."

Suddenly—I would even say miraculously—I started to breathe normally and come out of my death spiral. I pulled myself up off the floor, staggered outside, and dropped into a chair on the front patio, which overlooked the mountains of Colombia, South America. "I can't believe I'm alive," I said. "I can't believe I'm alive!"

As those words echoed through my mind, I knew instinctively that something bigger than me had spared my life. Today, I tell people that even though I was a violent, drug-smuggling addict, God heard my prayer.

He heard that prayer and continued chasing me with His unrelenting love.

There Is Hope!

It took several more years for me to stop running, at the age of twenty-six, and say, "OK, God, I've had enough. Take me. I'm exhausted."

Though I was still a young man, my body and mind were wasted. Having done volumes of heavy drugs for such a long time, I could barely talk. Despite earning a college degree and lacking only a couple of credits for a second, I struggled to string together two coherent sentences. The church that introduced me to Jesus didn't know what to do with me. So they put me in the kids' Sunday school class (age fifteen and under), and I sat there like a zombie. Most of the church people thought I was too far gone and wouldn't make it. But while I looked half dead on the outside, a fire was kindling deep inside and being kept alive by the Holy Spirit. I was the epitome of a junkie, but I was a saved junkie.

Fortunately, the Holy Spirit doesn't need much to work with, just a willing vessel. He specializes in restoring the broken and redeeming the years the enemy has stolen. God took in this strung-out zombie junkie right where I was. He gave me true life, set me on my feet, and put me on a new path—His path. Along the way He brought into my life my beautiful wife, Tiz, who's way above my pay grade.

Together, Tiz and I have raised a wonderful family and pioneered seven thriving churches across the globe, breaking racial and cultural barriers while seeing thousands of broken souls come to Jesus and be set free. God has given us an international teaching ministry through television and books to help Christians recognize their Jewish roots, and we have the honor of working closely with Israeli government agencies and leaders, making significant impact to raise awareness, support, and humanitarian aid for the people and nation of Israel. We have been in advisory meetings with President Trump on the Middle East and have met with top Israeli rabbis such as Rabbi Israel Meir Lau. Several of our friends and colleagues have been appointed to serve in the current avdministration of President Trump. We've also met Israeli political and military leaders, including the former minister of defense, General Yoav Gallant, and even Prime Minister Netanyahu.

God has given Tiz and me unusual favor, and these leaders

have opened their ears and hearts to us. This influence makes no sense in the natural, and that's really the point. *From Junkie to Jerusalem* is about what God can do in and through the least of us. It's a journey not only of experiencing miracles but also of being faithful with a little and watching God multiply the "loaves and fishes" we give Him.

Of course, the following pages also reveal the many difficulties and battles the Lord has brought us through. In that old church where people didn't believe I'd last, the Lord instantly and supernaturally delivered me from years of drug addiction. Yet the angry, violent nature that was handed down to me generationally took more time to heal—a lot more. That curse had to be broken. When it was, the truths we learned shaped one of our foundational teachings and impacted thousands.

That's how God works. And here's some really good news: He "shows no partiality" (Rom. 2:11, ESV). What He does for one person, He is equally willing to do for another—including you. A lot of the study we do is from the Hebrew language. In Judaism, people say that whenever you see or hear of a miracle in someone's life, it means you're next.

We have seen miracles, and we have done some overcoming. In Revelation 12:11, a voice from heaven declared, "They overcame [the enemy] by the blood of the Lamb and by the word of their testimony." *From Junkie to Jerusalem* is a testimony of hope and overcoming. We have told our story from the White House to the most violent prisons; from Portland, Oregon, to the Philippines; and from the world's back alleys to its most exclusive estates. Tiz and I have learned firsthand that when the Lord comes into people's lives, the down-and-out and the up-and-coming will never be the same again.

Regardless of your current condition, this God story offers hope to you or someone you love. Tiz and I wrote this book to let you know that no matter where you're from, what you're going through, or what your children are experiencing, God has miracles in the works. If you are breathing, you are not too far gone; He still has an amazing future that awaits you.

You'll soon see how this is Tiz's story as much as mine. Her life has been an amazing miracle of faith, obedience, overcoming, and God's faithfulness. She has so much encouragement and hope to share. Some years ago, when doctors gave Tiz an ovarian cancer diagnosis and only three months to live, she did not surrender to fear and despair. She pressed into the presence and promises of God and received her miraculous healing. Against all odds, almost six years have now passed, leaving her doctors baffled but inspired. Wherever Tiz goes, she radiates God's love, joy, and hope.

Our grandson Lion also received a devastating cancer diagnosis that crushed our world. His was a rare form of leukemia with very grim survival rates. His doctors said that even if Lion beat the odds, there could be serious long-term complications. We stood against all that, and the leukemia is now gone.

Just this past year, when Tiz's surgeon heard Lion's story, she was thankful. She had studied infant leukemia and had never known of a child who survived it. But "now I know one," she said.

We'll talk more later about Lion's amazing story and how God used his miracles and Tiz's to profoundly impact Israel. Only God could have orchestrated such outcomes.

Who Would've Thought?

Years ago, when I walked into that little church, nobody even talked to me because, in their eyes, I was a complete junkie and beyond hope. Despite them the Lord saw my heart. Man might look on the outside, but God looks on the inside. He can take you from wherever you are to a life beyond anything you can imagine. He wants to show you what happiness is, and He wants to give it to you. Yet God's happiness often looks different from the counterfeit version the world chases. His comes with the peace and fulfillment that reach beyond all circumstances and pass all understanding.

Therefore, this is a "who would've thought?" kind of book. Who would have thought that a junkie who could barely write his name would wind up writing books? Who would have thought that a drug addict who could hardly talk would speak to hundreds of thousands while pastoring churches, teaching Bible classes on a worldwide TV program, and conferring with world leaders on global affairs impacting Israel? Who would have thought that my voice pleading not to die fifty years ago would become a voice to bring hope and life to thousands of people around the world? Only God could do that!

Maybe your son or daughter is an addict and all hope seems lost. Maybe you're a junkie who can barely put two sentences together. That's OK. God sees you. Maybe you are homeless and need God to provide a place for you to get on your feet. Or perhaps you are living in a mansion that feels like a prison of fear and depression. Maybe the doctor gave you a life-altering diagnosis, or perhaps a family member received bad news. Wherever you are and whatever your circumstances, there is hope!

I gave my life to the Lord during the Jesus movement that rocked the culture of the sixties and early seventies. No one had seen anything like what happened then. God took a generation of ragtag, pot-smoking, wandering hippies and showed up in their lives with signs and wonders. Not too many in the religious crowd thought those young people would make it, but God knew.

Out of that group God raised up strong men and women of faith—Davids, Daniels, Esthers, and Ruths—leaders who impacted their families, businesses, schools, and the world. And you know what? It's happening again. The Holy Spirit is moving in fresh and powerful ways now. I believe the world is on the brink of another major outpouring, but it will be on an even greater scale than the Jesus movement. Other spiritual leaders are sensing it too. End-time prophetic pieces are coming together in the United States, the Middle East, and around the world.

A key part of the end-time picture is the coming worldwide revival. Yet it starts with one person at a time, inside the heart, just as it did with a lost junkie from South St. Louis. God wants you to be part of what He's doing. Regardless of the world's growing darkness and turmoil, the future remains bright with the Lord inside you. So travel with Tiz and me in *From Junkie to Jerusalem*, and let our miracle story become yours.

Chapter 1

ALL MEANS ALL

'D BEEN PLAYING outside, doing what most eight-year-old boys do, and time got away from me. I was just ten minutes late when I bolted into the house, but I might as well have been ten hours overdue, because my dad was waiting. When he punched me, he knocked the breath out of me and sent me to the floor, doubled over and coughing. As I tried scooting away from him, he kicked me in the chest and back like he was kicking a football. And he barked insults at me through the entire beating.

Soon I began to cry, and my mom ran from the kitchen to see what the commotion was about. When she saw me, she rushed to my side and went into full nurse mode. Mom had done some nursing work in the past, and she recognized the signs of trouble.

"We've got to get him to the hospital!" she said.

"Why?" my dad asked with a snarl.

"Because his ribs look broken," she said, glaring at him. "This is serious."

"I'm not spending a penny on that blankety-blank," he fumed. "You patch him up! You tape him."

Mom ran to get some sheets and then tenderly bound my chest to hold my ribs in place. Whenever I breathed or tried to move, the excruciating pain made me moan. It was clear that my dad resented how Mom was caring for me; he just shook his head the whole time.

Although the physical abuse I experienced while growing up was unimaginable, the emotional abuse was worse. One time before my younger brother was born I ran into the house and stopped dead in my tracks as I overheard my dad on the phone trying to give me away to an orphanage or some other facility. That moment was seared into my memory like a brand on a cowhide. "I don't want him here," my father barked, with his back to me. "I've already got one son. Can't you take him?"

Cold shudders wracked my body, and I staggered into my room, devastated. Collapsing to the floor, I wept. "He's always so mean, but now he doesn't even want me?"

I cried and cried, and when I ran out of tears, something inside me snapped. At that young age, I somehow managed to get a grip, and I told myself, "I don't care what anybody does. No one will ever make me cry again."

My dad realized I had overheard him, and yet he never tried to make things right. He just didn't care. He didn't want me, so I became an orphan in my own home.

The six of us were crammed into a little 850-square-foot flat on Cherokee Street in the inner-city neighborhood of South St. Louis. My two brothers and I shared one extremely small bedroom, my little sister had a bedroom to herself, and my parents had their room. The kitchen and living room were super tiny, with one even tinier bathroom that we all shared. We lived practically on top of one another, bumping elbows and heads, with our terrorizing father squarely in the middle of everything.

My father physically beat us kids, including my sister. Once, as my brother and I messed around at the supper table, my dad swung at me with his closed fist. I ducked, knocking my full plate on the floor. My dad made me crawl on my hands and knees to eat my food off the floor with no utensils, like an animal. That was more than sixty years ago, and I can still feel the humiliation and shame.

On another occasion in our little kitchen, my brother said something he shouldn't have. My dad responded by throwing a big, hot cup of coffee across the table, and it hit my brother in the face. He screamed as the coffee burned his flesh. Thankfully there were no permanent scars, at least not physical ones.

During another dinnertime episode, after my dad tried to hit me, I ran out the front door wearing nothing but shorts—no shoes and no shirt. My aunt Helen lived a couple of miles away. Even though I was still little, I ran all the way to her house. She called my worried mom and said, "We found him. He's here."

When I got home, my dad made me pay. He had his methods, like taking us kids to the basement and making us bend over and hold our ankles while he beat us with his belt. He'd hold us against the wall by our throats and punch us in the stomach and say, "If you flinch, I'll punch you again."

Things like that happened all the time, prodding me toward a deep-seated hatred of my father. It's no exaggeration to say that he was a monster who tore through our lives and left great damage in his wake. Mom, on the other hand, was our angel. A peacekeeper at heart, she tried to protect us and keep the family intact the best she could. There was rarely any peace, though, and she too lived as a victim, always in fear of my father's rage.

We kids didn't know everything that happened behind the scenes. But what we knew was plenty. I don't remember my father ever hugging any of us. He was just a mad, mean, horrible man. Yet if I showed you our family photos, you'd think we were a picture-perfect family. You know what they say: "Looks can be deceiving." My dad could be a nice guy to the world but a completely different man with us.

Life in the Hood

The streets of South St. Louis were just as violent—maybe more so—as our little home. I grew up in what we called "the hood." In those days you didn't call it a gang. It was more of a tight-knit neighborhood. It seemed like every other day, we'd be in a brutal street fight against some opposing hood. In that setting, my growing rage became a fierce weapon.

In hindsight I know that God repeatedly sustained and protected me by His sheer grace. I can't tell you how many times I should have died or been imprisoned. During one street fight, a guy broke a bottle and stabbed my buddy's face with the jagged glass, slicing his eye in half. When I saw that, I lost it. I grabbed the guy who did it, and I beat his head on the curb. Then, I took a brick and hit his head again, fully intending to kill him.

My anger was out of control. Amazingly, my victim survived (barely), but the police arrested me. Instead of charging me, however, they released me. Members of that guy's family had committed a series of more heinous crimes, and the police had been looking to put him and his whole family behind bars. When the authorities asked me to testify against him, though, I refused because snitching went against our street ethics. It was OK to almost kill someone, but snitching was out of bounds. That's how messed up we were!

Located in our neighborhood was the oldest high school west of the Mississippi. It was such a violent place that armed guards patrolled the property (which was a big deal back then). One day during classes, students from a rival school came and shot up our building. We heard *pa-pa-pa-pa-pa* as they fired on the front of the school. Everybody ran outside, and a brawl broke out. In our foolish rage, we ignored the fact that they were armed and we weren't.

That's the atmosphere in which I grew up. It was brutal. With all the violence I witnessed and suffered inside and outside my home, I grew more hardened and explosive every day. In time, I developed a reputation as someone nobody dared to cross.

Safe Outlets and a Hardening Heart

As I grew into my teens, one of my "safe" outlets was athletics. I was particularly drawn to boxing and football, which allowed me to vent my aggression in legal ways. Our coaches and trainers encouraged us in the hopes of keeping us off the streets as much as possible.

It so happened that I was pretty good at these two sports. I competed as a Golden Gloves boxer and ended up getting a full scholarship for football. At the Illinois Golden Gloves the first guy I fought was expected to win a medal in the Olympics. I knocked him out in fifty-four seconds of the first round. I guess my baby face had some folks fooled. The trainers asked, "Where's all that aggression coming from?"

The answer was simple. Whenever I fought, whether in the ring or on the streets, I always pictured my dad. I hated him that much. It wasn't a formula for success in life, but it helped me win fights.

During the couple of months between high school and college, I did a brief stint in jail for beating up some guy in a street fight. The police let me out but restricted me from leaving St. Louis for several weeks. At that time a military recruiter for the Green Berets heard about my violence and ability on the street. The Vietnam War was heating up, so he tried to talk me into joining the fight.

At first I was all in. I passed the military tests and physicals and was close to being sworn in. Then my travel ban was lifted, and I received a football scholarship offer. So I decided to skip the military and go to college. I was still on the military's radar, however. They recognized my violent nature and knew I could fight.

After (somehow) surviving my father's beatings, the local street violence, and some jail time, I was set to go away to college, about two hours down the Mississippi River. I saw college as my ticket out—and it was, but not the way I had imagined. When I came home for one of my first breaks, my thirteen-year-old sister met me outside. Her eyes were black and blue, and the whole side of her face was swollen. My dad had used her as a punching bag.

It was more than I could take. From outside, I screamed at my dad, who was in the house, "You get out here now! I'm going to kill you! You hear me? I'm going to kill you!"

I waited for a response and screamed again. "I told you to come out here! I'm going to kill you!"

By then our neighbors had gathered in their front yards to watch the spectacle. Finally, my dad yelled out the front door, "I'm calling the police! You better get out of here."

For the first time I detected a hint of fear in my father's voice. I left and crashed at a friend's house. About a year later I was in a car accident while riding with someone from college, and I was hospitalized for two weeks. My dad wouldn't let my mom or siblings visit me, so I was alone in the hospital. Can you imagine the impact on my self-worth? I felt I wasn't valued or loved enough to receive a visit from my own family.

When the hospital discharged me, the college was closed

for the Christmas holidays, so I caught a ride back to St. Louis with a friend. I called my mom from my friend's house and told her I was on my way home. "Well," she said, "I don't know if that's a good idea."

"I've got nowhere else to go, Mom," I said. "I'm coming."

My friend dropped me off a block from home, and I walked to the house. My dad knew I was coming and was waiting in the driveway. He saw me from a distance, but unlike the father of the prodigal son, he didn't run to me with his arms flung open. He didn't hug me and kiss my cheek. He didn't put his ring on my finger and say, "Go kill the fatted calf. Let's have a party!"

No. As I walked up the driveway, my father acted like he wanted a fistfight. He demanded, "What are you doing here?"

"It's Christmas. I came home."

"You don't have a home anymore," he said.

At least the prodigal had a home to return to. My dad's words could have crushed me, but instead they cemented my hardened, fractured heart. I turned around and walked away. It would be many years before I visited that house or saw my dad again. He never came to any of my college games, and he skipped my college graduation.

Desperately Seeking God

My journey from junkie to Jerusalem began long before I became a drug user. And although I ended up a full-blown addict, the anger and violence within me were just as toxic. As the story in these pages unfolds, you will see how the Lord chased me down with His persistent love and brought me home to my heavenly Father. That Father awaited me with arms wide open. As I ran from the long arm of the law,

I ran into the loving arms of the Lord, and He miraculously delivered me from drugs.

Still, the rage and violence that were embedded in my personality remained as strongholds and eventually bled into my marriage, family, and ministry. Even after I became born again and had the Holy Spirit living inside me, rage's bitter poison oozed out and tainted everything and everyone. One of my pastors saw my struggle and said, "Larry, you will have to learn to let God and people love you."

Doing that would prove to be a challenge. As our ministry exploded and thousands of both young and old people from the streets came to the Lord, it seemed that everyone was focused on how God delivered me from drugs. Although drugs had been my main problem and God's deliverance was undeniably supernatural, I had another issue: I was prone to extreme violence.

When my son, Luke (who is now my associate pastor), was around four years old, he did something rambunctious. I grabbed him and threw him against the wall, and he bounced off it like a football. Mind you, I was a pastor at this time. More importantly I was a father. Suddenly it felt like the Holy Spirit hit me between the eyes with a two-by-four and jolted me to my senses with this thought: "Larry, you are just like your dad."

The reality had never been starker. I had become what I despised. I knew that if the pattern continued, the dark hole that threatened to suck me into its depths and engulf me would also take from me the people I loved most. So I cried out to the Lord in repentance. I sought His face and wisdom. Then, I desperately dug into the Scriptures like a forty-niner digging for gold. I wanted to know whether the Bible talked about what a father passes on to his son.

My research was life-altering. The promise of Matthew 7:7 proved true: "Ask and keep on asking and it will be given to you; seek and keep on seeking and you will find; knock and keep on knocking and the door will be opened to you" (AMP). The Lord started teaching me from His heart. He showed me that family curses and generational curses are mentioned some 325 times in the Bible. I began studying the breaking of generational curses. I realized that Jesus not only died for my sin but also came to break those curses and the iniquity inside me.

Galatians 3:13 says, "Cursed is everyone who hangs on a tree." That truth led to a broader understanding of the seven places where Jesus shed His blood leading up to His death on the cross and how that not only freed us from sin but also won back our willpower, health, prosperity, joy, and more.[1] I said, "God, this rage is a curse in my life that must be broken."

I also began to understand why Moses wasn't allowed to enter the Promised Land. Some scholars believe it's because he never got over his anger. Moses killed an Egyptian in anger, and years later his anger caused him to strike the rock with his rod. (See Exodus 2:11–12; Numbers 20:10–11.) Like Moses I brought the spirit of anger into my faith, my marriage, and my family. God would use me, but He would not let me enter the fullness of my destiny as an angry person.

Ultimately, the strongholds of anger and violence came crashing down. The same power of God that set me free from drugs, alcohol, smoking, and all sin set me free from anger and violence. This was a turning point in my life. Eventually I would write a book about breaking generational curses. God used my deliverance from drugs to help thousands, but what He taught me about generational curses has helped tens of thousands because so many people can relate to the issue.

That is the power of the Holy Spirit! You can come to God with any sin. Nothing is too awful. God wants to deliver you from whatever can ruin your life. The chains won't always fall off the moment you are born again; some will come off in phases. Yet if you stay the course and keep your faith in Him, the Lord is always faithful. The enemy may have ripped you off in the past, but don't hand him your future. With the Holy Spirit you have the power to change any destructive behaviors. Through Christ the curse is broken, but you must choose the paths you will walk in.

A Golden Road

The apostle Paul explained that "we do not wrestle against flesh and blood, but against principalities, against powers" (Eph. 6:12). Grasping this truth was essential to the process of forgiving my dad. I had to realize that he had been abused and that he inherited his anger and violence.

My dad wasn't my enemy. The devil was. Knowing that my battle was not with flesh and blood but with principalities and powers, I was able to forgive my father. The Lord also helped me understand Matthew 6:14–15, which says, "If you forgive other people when they sin against you, your heavenly Father will also forgive you. But if you do not forgive others their sins, your Father will not forgive your sins" (NIV).

When Jesus taught His disciples how to pray, He said, "Forgive us our sins, for we also forgive everyone who sins against us" (Luke 11:4, NIV). To receive God's forgiveness for my sins, I had to forgive my dad's wrongdoing. When I did that, the Lord replaced the poison of my anger with His peace. I still didn't have much emotion toward my dad, but for many years before he died, I had peace in my soul and was able to make peace with him. My dad passed away in 2011, while Tiz and I were pastoring here in Dallas. A year before that, he prayed and gave his life to the Lord. Dad's transformation was evident and immediate. His hard demeanor softened as God did a work in his heart.

My dad spent his final days in a coma at a veterans' hospital in St. Louis. My siblings, mom, and I went there to be with him, and some other family members joined us. There were still many unresolved issues, raw emotions, and unhealed wounds in all of us. Yet somehow my heart went out to the man who had so damaged us. I don't know any other way to say it except that the hate was gone. Standing at his bedside, I realized that he was a broken, lonely human being, and I felt compassion for him.

On one of those days, I was at the hospital before anybody else arrived. The nurse came in and asked, "Aren't you the son who's a pastor?"

"Yes, ma'am, I am," I replied. "Listen, how long does somebody last like this?"

"Well, you never know," she said.

"Do they ever come out? Because I wanted to say something to him."

"Can I tell you something?" she asked.

"Sure."

"My mom was in a comatose state and was in a situation much like your dad's. She and her mom weren't close and had gone through a lot of hurt." The nurse continued, "We were gathered around Mom, telling her, 'We love you. We forgive you. If you're ready to go, you can go.' Then suddenly my mom popped out of the coma, sat up, stared straight ahead, and said, 'What's that golden road?' I asked her what she saw, and she said, 'There's a bright light down that golden road. I want to go. I want to go.' I said, 'Mom, go ahead and go. It's OK.' My mom lay back down and was gone."

Then the nurse returned to my question about Dad's coma. "We're not sure how long he has," she noted. "But we think that your dad can hear you, even though he's in a coma." She then walked out of the room.

I turned to Dad and said, "Listen, Dad, everything's fine. I have no hard feelings. I love you. We love you. If you're ready to go, you can go. Jesus is waiting for you." When I said that, I could almost see him sigh. Then he passed into eternity.

That whole year of my dad's salvation and reconciliation was an answer to decades of prayer. Never stop wrestling in prayer for the salvation of your loved ones. Sometimes it's a lifetime deal, but it's worth it. There were few tears at Dad's funeral, but there was forgiveness and reconciliation. Only Jesus could have done that.

And only Jesus could have saved me. Yes, I had been just like my father, but my father didn't know Jesus until the final year of his life. He didn't have the Holy Spirit working inside him before that. Only when the Spirit came to live inside him did transformation begin.

The Holy Spirit doesn't leave us as we are. Some issues take longer to resolve than others, but He is always working, conforming us to the image of Christ and using us for His purposes. It's a lifetime process. One thing is certain, though: No matter how long it takes, we can be "confident of this very thing, that He who has begun a good work in [us] will complete it until the day of Jesus Christ" (Phil. 1:6).

Romans 8:28–29 says, "We know that all things work together for good to those who love God, to those who are the called according to His purpose. For whom He foreknew, He also predestined to be conformed to the image of His Son."

Whatever it is—whatever sin, struggle, or misstep—if you give it to Him, He will deliver you and work it for your good and His purposes. This promise holds even if you're a junkie and a violent, angry person like I was. "All things" means *all* things. So believe it!

But what is God's purpose? Romans 8:29 says that He predestined those He foreknew "to be conformed to the image of His Son." If you are His, God is using everything in your life to make you more like Jesus. That is His purpose. Let Him work in you, knowing that it's a lifetime journey. When you stumble along the way or suffer a setback, just grasp His hand and let Him pull you back onto His path. He is faithful!

Chapter 2

THE ALL-AMERICAN

MY GROWING-UP YEARS were tough. I finally left home and the hood to play football and pursue my studies at Southeast Missouri State, the home of the mighty Redhawks. Cape Girardeau, a charming college town about two hours south of St. Louis, became home at this important time in my life. I weighed 212 pounds, with almost zero body fat. I was chiseled and clean-cut, with hair trimmed above my ears. Like most scholarship athletes, I felt like I was everybody's all-American guy looking to take the campus by storm. I was also the class clown, the life of the party, and a true party animal.

The problem was that underneath my all-American exterior was a deeply wounded young man. I was broke, both in soul and pocketbook. Not only had I grown up in an abusive atmosphere, but my family was what they call *dirt poor* in Missouri. I'm sure being poor played some part in my father's anger. He always struggled to make ends meet and came up short. My full-ride scholarship included room and board, for which I'm forever grateful. But there was no money for anything else except the barest necessities.

Until that point in my life, I mainly smoked pot with my friends. I shared the tokes but had not yet been drawn into any stronger drugs. Nor had I sold any drugs. Sports had pretty much been my focus. But this was the late sixties, and it seemed like everybody on campus was smoking pot and getting high, including many of my teammates.

Soon my pot smoking became more frequent and intense. Opportunities came to experiment with heavier stuff, which I was more than willing to try. My gravitation toward drugs was largely, and perhaps subconsciously, an attempt to quiet the raging voices within me. While I appeared to be strong and in control, I was confused and trying to convince myself that I mattered. Scraping and scratching around for drug money, I often did without life's essentials. However, as a popular athlete, I almost always found someone eager to help me out.

From Using to Dealing

It soon occurred to me that there was money to be made selling drugs—a lot of money for a struggling college student. "Why not me?" I reasoned. I knew how the system worked, and because of my reputation, I quickly made connections. So I pushed the illegality issue to the side. After all, I was Larry Huch, the tough-guy athlete who would never get caught.

I began my secret side business by selling marijuana, the drug that started my drug habit. Soon, however, my business expanded, and I was dealing acid and speed, which were in high demand. Dealing kept money in my pocket as I attended classes, went to football practice, and partied. I could be my own man and didn't need anything or anyone from my past. I kept my profile low among the coaches, although some of them knew what was going on behind the scenes. Amazingly, I remained competitive as an athlete.

Everything changed as the semesters passed and graduation came into view. My drug business continued growing, and my personal drug use morphed into full-blown addiction. I thought about almost nothing but my next high. Once you're an addict, the spiral into the abyss is both brutal and swift. You don't always recognize the tipping point until it is too late or you are too far gone to care. When you live for the next fix, you become less and less concerned about other things, including people. As they say, "Sin will take you farther than you want to go, keep you longer than you want to stay, and cost you more than you want to pay." That saying is never truer than when drugs are involved.

The fact that I was nearing graduation was a miracle all by itself. But I was associating with guys who were dealing in heavier stuff, particularly cocaine, which was taking over the drug scene. The cocaine high is fast and intense, giving users the instant euphoria that makes them feel like Superman or Wonder Woman. The downside is the crash, which is equally fast and intense. With each cycle, a deeper post-high depression creates an even more insatiable craving to be high again. The body's tolerance also develops quickly with cocaine, creating demand for higher and higher dosages to achieve the same euphoria.

This pattern is an addict's nightmare and a dealer's dream. I was dealing quite heavily around St. Louis and Cape Girardeau, making more money than I had ever made in my life. Yet, even then, God had His eye on me and pursued me, planting His seeds along the way.

Seedtime Comes

One day as I walked across the campus, I ran into a former teammate. He'd been one of our quarterbacks, a popular wild child with whom I'd done some heavy partying.

With a warm smile, he said, "Hey, man."

"What's up?" I replied.

Still grinning, he looked straight into my eyes, and I knew that something about him had changed. He handed me a pamphlet, and I looked down at it. "What's this?" I smirked.

"It tells how Jesus died for you, man." It was one of those gospel tracts that explains the plan of salvation. Turns out, he'd given his life to the Lord and was out witnessing on campus.

"What in the world?" was all I could say.

He just kept smiling and said, "Yeah, man. Jesus changed my life."

I laughed in his face and walked off. But you know what? The exchange pricked something in me. Like I said, I'd grown up with very little church background. My mom took us to church a couple of times before I was old enough to really remember it, but my dad put a stop to that. As I entered adolescence, my friends and I sometimes stayed out all night, roaming the streets and getting into trouble. By dawn we'd be cold and would go into the Catholic church to warm up. Sometimes we showed up during the early morning mass. I didn't know anything about religion, but I watched what the priests did. The *father* title always got to me, yet I thought, "Someday I'm going to know God. Someday." I had no idea where that thought came from, but I remembered it.

Now, on campus, I tucked the tract from my friend into my pocket. Something wouldn't let me get rid of it, and I always kept it with me. It was in my house for I don't know how long.

My drug buddies and I would smoke dope, look at the tract, and talk about it. We all knew the former quarterback who gave it to me, and we thought the change in him was odd. We laughed because it reminded us of a popular Elton John song that talked about Jesus freaks handing out stuff to passersby.[1]

Giving someone a gospel tract might seem foolish to some, but God uses those things. Paul wrote, "It pleased God through the foolishness of the message preached to save those who believe" (1 Cor. 1:21). He later added, "I planted, Apollos watered, but God gave the increase. So then neither he who plants is anything, nor he who waters, but God who gives the increase. Now he who plants and he who waters are one, and each one will receive his own reward according to his own labor" (3:6–8). That tract and conversation, as odd as they were, planted a seed that God would later water.

Taking the Bait

My family was so poor that my gift for being the first-ever Huch to graduate from college was a white shirt and a tie. I'd earned a teaching degree with a double major so I could teach anything from kindergarten through twelfth grade, and I qualified for coaching positions. When I did my student teaching, the fourth-grade kids I taught loved me. I came to school wearing long hair and riding a 1969 Triumph Bonneville chopper I got in exchange for a couple of bags of dope. Teachers couldn't get away with such things today, but I rewarded the kids by taking them outside for class. If they got their homework done, I'd give them motorcycle rides around the parking lot. Some parents said, "Man, my kids never loved school so much." The district supervisor told me, "The job is yours if you want it."

After I graduated, however, life became all about money and getting high. It's not as though job prospects were lacking. Even companies outside my major were interested in me. I had been a good athlete, and firms wanted hires with that kind of discipline. But I was making good money selling drugs, and I knew there was a whole lot more money to be made if I worked at it.

Because I was a tough street guy, some of my dealer friends who weren't as streetwise told me, "Listen, you're not afraid, and you can handle yourself on the streets. Why don't you go down to Colombia, find the cocaine, buy it cheap, and ship it directly to us? We'll be your contacts here. We'll cut out the middleman and make a fortune."

"I'm listening," I said.

Up till then, the cocaine we sold was first smuggled in from South America by middlemen. To get our supply, we had to give them a cut. We realized that we could make ridiculous amounts of money by going around them. That meant I would be the guy on Colombia's streets who purchased high-quality cocaine at a low price, smuggled it into the United States, and shipped it to American dealers I could trust.

It seemed like the perfect plan, and because I grew up with nothing, I took the bait. "Money's where it's at," I told myself, "and I'm going to do whatever it takes to make a lot of it."

So off I went to Colombia.

Chapter 3

THE MYSTERIOUS MAN
ON THE PLANE

STILL MUSCULAR AND tough, I knew there were risks involved in going to Colombia—serious risks. Nonetheless, my young, dauntless mind was made up. This was my chance to make it big, and I was ready to go.

By then I had a reputation, and because of my connections, word got out to certain people in Colombia that I was coming. A friend of mine planned to fly down with me—not to set up the drug trade but to soak up the party scene and the endless supply of cocaine. He didn't have a clue about the hornet's nest we were about to enter. Neither did I.

The timing seemed perfect. The demand for psychoactive drugs exploded during the sixties and seventies, and Colombia became the world's leading producer of coca, the main ingredient for illegal cocaine. The coca plant grows almost exclusively in northern and western parts of South America. Its leaves produce a surge in serotonin and dopamine, producing an intense high.[1]

We were scheduled to fly from Miami to Medellín, Colombia, then a jam-packed city of more than a million people nestled in the Andes Mountains' Aburrá Valley. Medellín was a beautiful and vibrant place, with Spanish/Caribbean charm, but it was also extremely dangerous. The cartels were everywhere, controlling everything from hotels to nightclubs and from the cab system to the police.

As a self-assured twenty-three-year-old, I felt the need to be in the middle of the danger, seeking a connection so I could smuggle cocaine into the United States. I thought I was invincible. So my friend and I got our passports and tickets and boarded a jet bound for Medellín. We must have looked like we hitched a ride straight from Woodstock. I, for one, sported a long goatee, and my wild hair reached past my shoulders. I wore shades, and the number of my tattoos was growing along with my hair.

As we sat way back in coach, chilling out and awaiting takeoff, the flight attendant walked up and said, "Excuse me. Are you Larry Huch?"

I froze for a second, thinking, "Am I in trouble already?" Then I answered, "Yes, ma'am."

She said, "Well, we've got a seat reserved for you in first class."

"You do?" I responded, surprised. "First class? There must be some mistake."

"Not if you're Larry Huch."

Just like that, they bumped me up to the first-class cabin where a mysterious Colombian man awaited me. He smiled and nodded for me to sit. I eased into the seat beside him, not sure what to make of his generosity. He seemed to be in his fifties. His attire was sharp but casual, and he introduced himself as Luis, a businessman who traveled back and forth from Colombia to the States. We both knew what that meant but dared not say it aloud. I thanked him for his gift, and we engaged in small talk.

Though he seemed kind, I played it safe, keeping my plans close to the vest. We both played the game, sizing each other up and feeling each other out. Luis asked, "Where in Medellín are you staying?"

"A cheap, local hotel," I said.

"No, no," he said, "that's not a good area. You need to come and stay at a hotel that a friend of mine owns."

"Thanks for the offer," I replied. "But that's OK. We're good." I realized he could be a narc, setting me up. He nodded with a smile as the jet's engines engaged, and we started down the runway. I laid my head back, closed my eyes, and thought, "Why is this man being so nice to me?" I had an idea that something was up.

Hello, Medellín

Luis and I kicked back in our seats for most of the three-and-a-half-hour flight. When we finally landed in Medellín and were about to deplane, Luis whispered in my ear, "Stay quiet, and come with me."

When my traveling companion and I reconnected and did what Luis said, customs agents waved the three of us through. Outside by the curb, not one car but two awaited us. "You ride with me," Luis said, "and we'll put the luggage and your friend in that car." He made it clear that he wanted to separate my friend and me as much as possible. I still thought Luis might be a narc, but I was becoming more certain that he was part of the cartel. For some strange reason I trusted him, and we climbed into one of his vehicles.

En route to our hotel we passed a super-luxurious five-star resort, and Luis said, "That's the place my friend owns. You can stay there."

Tempted by the offer but holding firm, I said, "No, thank you."

"OK, whatever you want."

With that, Luis dropped us off at our hotel and went on his way. I figured he'd pop up again somewhere. He did, sooner than I expected.

Not thirty minutes later my friend and I heard a knock at our hotel room door. It was Luis. "Come," he said, motioning excitedly with his hands. "I'll show you around town."

I remained hesitant. "What's this guy up to?" I wondered. "I mean, a first-class seat, waved through customs, two cars waiting, a ride to the hotel, and an offer to stay at a five-star resort? Now he's offering me a tour of Medellín, which is a big city. Something is definitely up."

For all I knew, he could be taking me to an abandoned warehouse to interrogate me and dump me in a jungle river somewhere. But I was the invincible tough guy who could handle anything. So I left behind my travel companion and cooperated with whatever Luis had in mind. Curious about where the adventure would lead, I decided to do nothing that might set off Luis or incriminate me, in case he was working undercover.

I got into his car, and he drove us around Medellín, pointing out the sights. He said, "Listen, you don't want to go into that area over there. It is owned by a certain drug cartel family." I stayed mostly quiet, nodding as he drove along. "And you never want to go into that section," he said, pointing. "But this area over here is OK."

On and on we drove, through section after section, with Luis giving me a detailed layout of the city. Like I said, I played it close to the vest and hadn't disclosed that I'd come to find cocaine to smuggle into the States. But Luis already knew.

Someone had obviously tipped him off so he could meet me on that plane in Miami. But who was it?

Then Luis took me to a big, beautiful high-rise surrounded by other gorgeous high-rises. He told me that his mother owned the whole tenth floor. "Yeah," he explained, "I bought this for my mom because I live mostly in the States and travel back and forth so much."

"Impressive," I thought to myself.

Then Luis took me to meet his mother. She was probably in her late seventies or early eighties—a very beautiful woman for her age. "Please, have some coffee," she said in Spanish.

Having never drunk coffee before, I replied in English, "No, thank you."

"No, no," Luis responded. "Drink it in her honor. It is an insult to refuse."

"OK," I said. And that was when I got hooked on coffee. There's nothing like pure Colombian coffee, and Luis' mother made what seemed like the best in the world.

After a nice visit with his mom, Luis took me back to my hotel and then checked in on me every day. A week or so later, I learned that he was indeed working with the drug cartel to vet me. If they decided they didn't want to do business with me, they had ways of making me disappear. Being both daring and foolish, I wasn't worried. My friend and I were having a good time partying in clubs and getting high. In the meantime, I attempted to make connections where I could, not knowing who to trust or distrust.

Medellín was a vibrant metropolis, and other Americans partied there. Yet my travel buddy and I never blended in. The reasons were easy to understand. Picture two white, long-haired, Missouri hippie dudes being dropped in the middle of the Colombian culture. Anyone could tell we had an agenda, or at least I did. I wasn't just a typical American wanting to party and do drugs. I had a distinct agenda and purpose. My addiction had not yet taken a heavy toll on my body. I was still buff and had obvious anger and aggression issues. I worked my plan, and the drug connection suppliers were working their plans, and our paths crossed. At that point in my life, making money was my goal, and I had never seriously contemplated my moral or spiritual state. Yet I had a strange sense that something bigger than me was at work in my life. I just didn't know who or what. I know now that those were senses of forces of good and evil—light and darkness—that were trying to influence my path and future.

Not too long afterward, while doing the party scene, I ran into a famous, wealthy, ex-bullfighter, or maybe he ran into me. Either way, he seemed to take a liking to me. The two of us started hanging out. He owned a good bit of prime real estate, including a radio station and an upscale hotel, where he graciously gave my friend and me a place to stay. In addition to real estate, he was—surprise, surprise—smuggling cocaine and looking for more connections into the States.

Someone had tipped off the ex-bullfighter as to why I was in Medellín. The drug-smuggling business was like the oil trade: The more pipelines you had, the more money you made. Our friendship had turned into a potential partnership where I would be one of his pipelines, traveling back and forth from the States to Colombia. We began planning how to smuggle coke into different American cities, including Los Angeles, where we could sell it to Hollywood entertainment types. Of course, I would continue supplying my contacts in the St. Louis area too.

What I didn't know was that other people were arranging for me to work with a different drug cartel family who wanted to separate me from my ex-bullfighter friend. I wasn't sure if Luis and the bullfighter were working together or against each other. I had no way of knowing who to trust, who was for me, or who was against me. I was in the middle of a vicious, power- and money-hungry, bloodthirsty group of people but was beginning to be aware of the dangers that I was in.

I was scared, but I was also ecstatic to be in the midst of such an adventure. Rather than run away from it in fear, I ran deeper into it in a fervor. That's how crazy, driven, and unhinged I was. I was in the middle of one of the biggest conflicts in the world at that time, where the drug wars were bursting from—Medellín, Colombia.

One day, while my travel companion was gone, the ex-bullfighter and I were in the hotel working out the next steps for our business. Suddenly, we heard pounding on the door—*bam, bam, bam!*

"Oh no," I thought, "I've been set up!"

I opened the door to find Luis standing there with a panicked look on his face. He hadn't been around for a while, as though he'd fallen off the map. "You've got to get out of here right now!" he shouted. "Right now!"

From the Metropolis to the Mountains

Luis shared some news that convinced me I was in a tough spot. "I've got a ranch in the mountains where you'll be safe," he added. "It will be good for your business too."

After what Luis had told me, I didn't hesitate to leave. I parted ways with the ex-bullfighter and fled to the mountains outside rural Envigado. Today, Envigado is a sprawling metroplex that bleeds into Medellín, but back then it was a quaint town with historic Spanish architecture, a picturesque square, and chickens running in the streets.

Envigado also happens to be where Pablo Escobar, the notorious leader of the Medellín cartel, started out. He arguably became the world's wealthiest and most powerful drug trafficker and was dubbed the King of Cocaine.[2] Escobar was vicious, and I happened to be there just as he was establishing a foothold. Fortunately, the Lord's protection was all around me, even when I didn't know it.

I'm skipping some details here, but I joined several others who lived and worked on Luis' Spanish-style ranch, known as a *finca*. Among them were some Colombian laborers and two other Americans who wanted some of the smuggling action—a guy and a girl whom we'll call Janet and Bruce, both hippie types around my age. The man who oversaw the ranch lived in another, smaller house with his wife and family. Janet, Bruce, and I connected almost instantly, and the three of us realized that we could help each other.

When I say *ranch*, you can assume that it wasn't being used to raise horses. In the nearby jungle, pure-cut cocaine was harvested and mixed, then brought to the ranch to be packaged. Each time a plane flew in via the airstrip in the jungle, we would run to meet it and load it with the coke. This kind of operation is portrayed in movies such as *American Made*, *Escobar: Paradise Lost*, and *Blow* and the Netflix series *Narcos*.[3]

Everyone at the ranch worked together, and the cartel groomed Janet, Bruce, and me to become traffickers who would develop routes in the United States. The cartel also permitted us to take some of the uncut cocaine and sell it directly to Americans for our own finances. It was very pure grade and much stronger than anything available in the States, so Americans willingly paid a fortune for it.

As a kind of training camp, living on the ranch gave us ringside seats to the operations. We saw planes and helicopters coming and going, and we had as much cocaine, marijuana, and alcohol as any user could possibly want. We used it, all right, and we were stoned all the time.

Meeting with the Cartel

After laying the initial groundwork for the smuggling operation, the cartel arranged our first official face-to-face meeting. They sent a car from their own cab company, called Estrellas (Spanish for "stars"), to pick Janet, Bruce, and me up from the ranch. Two very strict rules of the game were that (1) we were *never* to use another cab company, and (2) no one else was allowed up the mountain. The cabs were critical to the cartel's operations, as they were used to launder money and transport important associates. The TV series *Narcos* shows how Escobar laundered money and drugs through his cab drivers.

The Estrellas cab drove us to Envigado's little town square to meet the man who was running the cartel. He and three of his henchmen were inside a café, but they made us sit outside where they could watch us. They also didn't want to sit with us because word was out that three CIA or DEA agents were in town looking for somebody.

For the record I can't say with absolute certainty that the cartel head across the café was Escobar, but I'm now 95 percent sure it was him. At that point I had never seen him or heard his name. The cartel went to great lengths to prevent anyone from taking pictures of us together. So he stayed out of our sight and had a messenger walk back and forth between our tables to relay his messages and our responses.

During our meeting, as we were fully engaged in discussing business details, someone rushed into the café, grabbed the cartel head, and ushered him out. A car pulled up, received him, and sped off. A remaining cartel representative instructed Janet, Bruce, and me to take the Estrellas cab and return to the ranch immediately. "Those three agents are around here somewhere—two males and a female," they said. "So don't talk to anybody."

Dangerous Decisions

It didn't occur to us until later that we were two males and a female. As we three crossed the street to get in the cab, Bruce said, "You know, so-and-so outside of Medellín is having a party. Let's go check it out. Why go back to the ranch at three o'clock in the afternoon?"

Janet and I agreed, which meant disobeying the direct order we had received. It was a dumb move, but we were high enough for our judgment to be impaired. After we checked out the party scene and the sun began to set, we decided to head to the ranch. The drive from the party back to Envigado took thirty minutes. However, we still had to drive up a winding jungle road without streetlights, where it was scary dark. We called a taxi—but not the Estrellas cab we had been told to use (our second dumb move of the day).

Just as our driver headed down the street, a car with three Colombian men pulled up beside us. They began to scream and cuss at us, but we had no clue why. As impaired as we were, however, we knew something wasn't right. Our driver abruptly whipped the tiny car off the main road and went up a back road that turned to dirt. Janet was in the front seat because she spoke better Spanish than either Bruce or I did. In the back seat we started to panic. "Where are you taking us?" we yelled. "Get us back to Envigado!"

The driver yelled, "This is a shortcut! This is a shortcut!"

"No, no, get us back on the main road!" we shouted. But the driver ignored us.

About that time the two-guys-and-a-girl problem dawned on us. Somebody must have thought we were the three CIA or DEA agents who were supposedly working the area. Now in full-blown panic mode, we screamed, "No! Turn around! Take us to Envigado."

Everything on the dirt road was pitch black, except for some dim headlights ahead. From another dirt road off to the side, a car pulled out in front of us just as a second car pulled behind us. The car in front slowed to a crawl, and the car in back rode our bumper. We were sure they had come to kill us because they thought we were the three agents. So we screamed again, "Go! Pass him! Turn around!"

The driver refused and kept going in the same direction. We argued back and forth for ten or fifteen minutes, all of us screaming at the tops of our lungs. The cars that wedged us in kept it up.

The violent streak deep within me started rising up. Bruce leaned over and said in a quiet voice, "They're going to kill us. He's setting us up. We've got to kill this guy. We got to kill him."

I agreed. Since we weren't carrying our weapons, I took off my belt and got ready to kill the driver so we could take control of the car and get out of there. With milliseconds to spare before I committed murder, we came over a rise and saw Envigado just ahead. The two cars that had boxed us in took off in opposite directions, and the cab driver's life was spared.

The rattled driver stopped the car. We insisted that he take us up the road to the ranch, but he refused, saying, "No, no, no. I can't go up there. Nobody's cab is allowed up there."

"You have to go," we pleaded. "The ranch is a couple of miles away, and the road is dark."

"No," the driver said. "I cannot go. The drug cartel owns that road." He refused to defy the cartel, and he left us right there, in the dark.

We were still freaked out and unsure of what was happening. We had no choice but to walk the jungle mountain road in the middle of the night. Because we had no weapons, we carried rocks, fully expecting danger ahead. That night taught us to always carry weapons. But I'm thankful we didn't have any at the time. If we had, that poor driver would have died.

We eventually made it back to the ranch completely exhausted but relieved to be home. The fact that I'd almost killed the cabbie shook me to my bones. As I laid my head on my pillow that night, I thought, "Man, this anger thing is out of control. I'm going to kill someone and end up in prison."

I was scared stiff, but I refused to let it show. After some tossing and turning and very little sleep, I awoke and scratched around for a needle.

Chapter 4

PEBBLES IN MY SHOE

AFTER MORE THAN a year in and out of Colombia, I was deeply entrenched in drug trafficking. I even flew back and forth to do drug pickups in the States and to get things established with people there. The cartel's intention behind the smuggling scheme was to eventually force me to relinquish my passport in order to stay under the radar of the CIA and the US law enforcement. They planned to put the company in my name so we could export items stuffed with cocaine into the States.

We loaded contraband onto planes, boats, trucks—you name it. The cartels were raking in so much cash that they bought airplanes and were preparing to buy more. In the end, it was cheaper to buy a used 737, load it with cocaine, land it on a desolate airstrip, unload the drugs, and permanently abandon the plane. Of course, connections had to be set up in key locations beforehand so the shipments could be met and readied for distribution.

Because I was flying back to the States more often, I secured a remote cabin in the woods several miles outside Cape Girardeau, Missouri. It gave me a place to crash near St. Louis and allowed me to continue working my established areas. However, the bulk of my time was still spent on the ranch in Colombia. Having access to all the pure uncut cocaine we wanted was a major temptation for us junkies. Naturally, we saw unlimited access not as a problem but as the ultimate gift. Cocaine seemed to give us boundless energy and creativity, making us feel superhuman.

Living to get high, we did cocaine from the moment our eyes opened in the morning until we took our downers to sleep at night. We went to the store high, ate meals high, and did our work high—that is, until we crashed. Then it got ugly. To avoid the crash, I used drugs continuously, trapped in an endless, addictive cycle. I soon graduated from snorting all day to mainlining all day—putting the powder in a needle and shooting it straight into my veins. Eventually I had to shoot up ten or twelve times a day, which caused my veins to collapse.

The drugs wreaked havoc on my body and mind. I mentioned that when I first arrived in Colombia, I was still built of rock-hard muscle. After months of increased drug use, I was emaciated, weighing barely 145 pounds. Janet and Bruce, who were addicts themselves, were worried about me. That's how bad off I was.

Along with my heavy chemical dependency, I partook of all the immoral activities that seemed to accompany it. I had more money than I'd ever seen before. I thought that would make me as happy and free as an Andean condor soaring in the Colombian skies. But instead, I was bound up in my soul's dark abyss, which seemed to get deeper every time I came down from a high. The strangest thing, however, was a curious internal tug to find out who God was. It wouldn't let up but only grew more and more intense. My quandary was in not knowing what I was looking for. Was it God? And if so, what or who was God? Was He a force or a being?

Yes, I was a junkie, but I was an educated one. I knew that something—a speck of dust or a single cell—could not come out of absolutely nothing. For something or anything to exist, there had to be something that always was, whether it was matter or God. Way down deep, I knew the answer was God. But why was I here? Why did I exist?

I wasn't thinking about religion or even Christianity. I knew very little of that except what I already mentioned about the old Catholic church in my neighborhood, my precious aunt Helen, and the words that my quarterback friend shared: "You'll never find what you're looking for until you find Jesus."

I thought, "Surely, that can't be the answer." It seemed too simple. I thought I was looking for something more profound, more transcendental and mystical than "Jesus loves me, this I know, for the Bible tells me so." Yet thoughts of God—whoever He was—wouldn't leave my mind. Like pebbles in a shoe, they would have to be dealt with or I would have no peace.

Little did I know that the Holy Spirit was the irritant. Once He got my attention, He drew me in bit by bit, but it would take some time. The wild thing was that the more cocaine I used as an escape, the more I became aware of the tug. Cocaine didn't affect me the way drunkenness did. I felt like I was floating on air, but I wasn't out of it. Instead, I experienced a heightened sensitivity to whatever was going on.

I reasoned that in this state I would somehow discover who God was. Though the Lord would use the situation, what I thought was reason was a lie from the enemy. The father of lies is also a thief who knows all about stealing, killing, and destroying. (See John 10:10.) And drugs are one of the chief weapons he uses to open users to counterfeit entities, the demonic realm, and ultimately death.

Janet apparently saw that death was coming for me. She kept saying, "Larry, I'm really concerned about you. You're not eating, and you're using way too much."

I was annoyed by her mothering, and when she and Bruce went into town for groceries, I thought, "Now's my chance to load up and get *really* high."

That was when I doubled my dose three times and missed my vein on the first two tries. As I said in the preface, my third try nearly exploded my heart out of my chest, and I thought I was a dead man. Fifty years later, I remember that experience as though it happened this morning. I begged God not to let me die, and He answered my prayer.

A 1969 Ford Mustang Mach 1

Right around that time we had a shipment bound for the United States that would first be flown into Mexico. My job was to fly back to the States and then drive from my Missouri cabin to Mexico City to meet the shipment. Then I would turn it over to the next "leg" for distribution across the border. The plan called for a lot of work and driving, but the payoff would be worth the trouble. The cut from one shipment could keep me set for quite a while.

Each time I returned to the States for a stint like this, I lived with a woman around my age who occupied the cabin in my absence. For this trip I planned to pick her up so we could enter Mexico as a couple. She didn't have a passport, but that was not a problem. In those days Mexico was a fairly easy country to enter with only some documentation papers, which she had. So the two of us hopped in my yellow 1969 Ford Mustang Mach 1 and drove the thirtyish hours to Mexico City.

Whether I drove a motorcycle or a car, I always tried to have a cool ride. What's bizarre is that, decades later, the television program *Narcos* showed Colombian dealers interacting with someone in the United States driving a yellow '69 Mach 1. When Tiz and I watched the show, we looked at each other and said, "Wow! Can you believe that?" Because I had been selling to an undercover agent when I drove that exact make, model, and color of car, we had no doubt about why *that* car was on the screen.

My girlfriend and I drove into Mexico through Tijuana, where we knew the authorities would wave us into the city without an inspection. A little further into Tijuana, however, there was another checkpoint where a passport or papers would be required. I gave them my passport, but when my girlfriend dug through her stuff, she couldn't find her papers. She had assumed they were in her bags, but somehow they weren't.

Replacing the papers wasn't a huge problem. We simply needed to turn around, cross back into the States, and get new paperwork in any town. But entering the United States would not be as easy as entering Mexico had been. We would face an inspection, and because I knew we wouldn't be checked while crossing into Mexico, I had my personal stash with me, including all my cocaine and now some heroin for my new speedballing habit. The combination of cocaine and heroin gave me an extra high but was potentially lethal. I had fallen so far down the junkie hole that I could not function without a dangerous fix.

There was no crossing back into the United States with all that contraband, so I whipped the Mustang around to a Tijuana side street and looked for someplace to hide my stuff. A little off the main path, I spotted one of those heavy city trash cans. I pulled over and jammed my stash under the can, making certain it was secure and completely covered. I thought, "We won't be long, and who's going to dig under a heavy trash can?"

My thinking seemed logical at the time. Now I reflect on decisions like that and scratch my head. In any case, we cruised through the border checkpoint and easily got new paperwork in the United States. But when I returned to the trash can, my drugs were gone. For the first time in more than a year, I had nothing to shoot up. I didn't have the time or money at that moment to locate a dealer because I had to meet the incoming cocaine shipment. Once I did that, I would have all the cocaine I needed.

But first I would endure a tough drive to Mexico City. Without a fix my body started trembling, and my nerves went haywire. I was in the early stage of withdrawal. I pounded the steering wheel as my anger escalated. I thought, "Man, I'm not in a good place. This addiction is serious!"

It *was* serious, and my situation was about to get worse. My girlfriend and I reached Mexico City, but the shipment did not. My withdrawal symptoms were getting worse, so we bought some marijuana and liquor to ease the edge until the shipment came. It never showed up. I called one of our transporters in Colombia to see what was going on. He said, "Bro, the shipment should be there."

Starting to panic, I repeatedly tried to reach Janet and Bruce at the ranch, without success. Finally, I contacted the señor and señora who were the family over the ranch. They informed me that bandits had come the night before. The thieves robbed them, held them at gunpoint, put a gun to señor's head, and pulled the trigger. Thankfully, the gun misfired. The victims started screaming, and the workers started running. The bandits intended to murder them, but somehow they didn't.

Because we dealt in cash, tens of thousands of dollars were hidden throughout the ranch. The workers showed the bandits where the money was, and the thieves took off with it. The shipment got messed up, the money was stolen, and Janet and Bruce were missing. Word was they might have been kidnapped. Whether they were or not, I don't know. I never heard from them again.

My girlfriend and I drove all the way back to my cabin in Missouri. Miraculously, we arrived safely. I say *miraculously* because I had to fight withdrawal the whole way. I found some cocaine in the cabin and shot up, which returned me to my calm junkie self.

Another shipment of drugs was already en route to St. Louis. Before going to pick it up, I discovered that my girlfriend was involved with some stuff that I wanted no part of. So I dumped her and then left to meet the shipment of contraband. That delivery arrived. With the drugs in hand I drove back to the cabin, satisfied to know I'd have a fix when I needed it.

At that point I was taking enough drugs to send me to jail for a long time if they were confiscated. And still I felt invincible.

When I returned to the cabin around 1 a.m., I found the place ransacked. Stuff was turned upside down and flung everywhere. Fortunately my now ex-girlfriend wasn't there. Scanning my raided cabin on my own, I figured that somebody had come looking for drugs. They'd been tipped off, but by whom?

I called a friend of mine in the area. He answered, and almost before I could say "Hello," he asked, "Dude, where are you? What's going on?"

"Man, I just came in from St. Louis."

"The cops are looking for you," he said. "They made a major

drug bust of the whole area. They hit everybody at five minutes to midnight."

Forty-eight people had been arrested. If I had arrived an hour earlier, that number would have been forty-nine.

Mom Shows Up

For years my mother never told anybody where I lived because she feared they would come and arrest me. When people asked about me, she'd say, "Oh, Larry's living in Wyoming," or "He's living in Montana."

This time, when I returned from Colombia, Mom heard that I was back, and she drove down from St. Louis to find me. She inquired around the area, and someone who knew me said, "He's living in this cabin out in the woods."

Mom found my place in the sticks, stepped onto the creaky porch, and knocked on the dilapidated door. She had no idea whether I'd be there, and I had no idea that she was coming.

When I opened the door, I shouted, "Mom!" and she just burst into tears. The last time she'd seen me, I looked like an all-American collegiate athlete. Now I weighed 145 pounds. I had black bags under my eyes, needle marks covered my arms, and my hair dangled past my shoulders. Years later she told Tiz, "When I left Larry that day, I thought I would never see him alive again. He'd either get killed in a drug deal or an overdose, because 'once a junkie, always a junkie.'"

When Mom saw me in that condition, she said, "You're coming home with me. You're coming back home."

"I'm not, Mom," I told her. "Besides, Dad won't let me back."

Mom eventually relented, and I would not see her again for several years—not until after the Lord came into my life.

A Package from Aunt Helen

One day I cruised over to the post office on my chopper and found a letter from my aunt Helen along with a Bible she'd given me when I was five years old. Like I said, my mom took us to church only a couple of times. But Aunt Helen was a strong Christian and a wonderful, loving person. Like my mom, my aunt is one of my favorite people in the world, and she never gave up on me. Most everyone believed I'd always be a junkie. I guess Aunt Helen believed that "if the Son makes you free, you shall be free indeed" (John 8:36).

Aunt Helen's letter got right to the point: "Larry, I was praying," she wrote, "and I really believe the Lord said that this is your time to give your life to Jesus."

As I read those words, my mind raced through the details of my next drug deal. I said to myself, "Aunt Helen is so sweet," and didn't think anything more about it.

Once I was back at the cabin, I got high all that day and into the evening. When I tried to sleep, I couldn't, so I clicked on my little black-and-white TV. In those days, there were only three channels where I lived, and two of them went off the air after midnight. The only thing still on was a preacher. I can't remember whether it was Billy Graham or Oral Roberts. It could have been Jesus, and I wouldn't have known the difference.

Whoever it was said, "You're sitting there right now, and you're saying to yourself, 'I am so sick and tired of living this way.'" Then he said, "Jesus is what you're looking for. Why don't you get on your knees right where you are and ask God to help you?"

So I did. Right there, I dropped to my knees and said, "God, help me. I know I'm a mess. I know 'once a junkie, always a junkie,' but please help me."

I felt something but didn't know what it was—maybe a stirring of hope at the possibility that I didn't have to live the same way forever. Even though the preacher said, "Jesus is what you are looking for," I still didn't understand who or what God was. What is certain is that I cried out to Him for a second time on this journey. My experience that night was one of the reasons I knew years later that television reaches people and that it would play a major role in our ministry.

———•———

After my return from Mexico City, the authorities watched my every move. An undercover source got this message to me: "Larry's number two on the list. You'd better tell him to be careful." To arrest me, the authorities had to catch me in the act of selling. But after the raid on my cabin and the drug busts in the area, selling had come to an abrupt halt. I didn't know what I was going to do or what my future held. So I decided to lay low for a while—sort of. But the Holy Spirit never stopped chasing me. Those darn pebbles in my shoe held my attention.

Chapter 5

I COULDN'T LIFT MY ARMS

OR THE TIME being, my drug dealing days were over, both in Colombia and St. Louis. My cash flow was cut off like water in a kinked hose. But my addiction was becoming more and more demanding, forcing me to sell my valuables, including my cherished 1969 Mustang Mach 1. That really hurt, but addiction doesn't care about your pain. Drugs are cruel taskmasters. As your habit costs more and more, you're locked out of the job market because you're a junkie.

At least I still had my Harley-Davidson chopper to get me around. Can you picture this hippie dude cruising around on that hog with his long hair, Fu Manchu mustache, tattoos, and sunglasses? That was me. I wanted to be free and tried to reflect that image, yet I was far from free. My addiction and my angry, violent nature were both out of control. At times I wanted to quit using drugs, but I was truly driven to conquer my anger and violent nature. I had no peace, and I feared what I was becoming, although I'd never admit it to anyone.

Inner turmoil plagued me all during the hippie peace movement. I searched for a path to peace and got involved in transcendental meditation. It was my first attempt to rehabilitate myself, and I was serious about it. I dove headfirst into my new lifestyle, becoming a vegetarian, baking my own bread, doing meditation sessions several times a day, studying, and seeking out yogis. I was willing to do whatever it took to break my anger. I hated being violent, and interestingly enough, I felt like only God could help me. Yet at this point, I read and sought every spiritual source except the Bible.

Two Friends, My Eric, and a Bully

During that time I had two friends who happened to be women (go figure). Kim and Rhonda were close, like sisters. I started a relationship with Kim. She lived with me, but the three of us began hanging out together. We were almost inseparable, and Kim's Volkswagen van came in handy.

I haven't mentioned it, but I'm a dog lover. I had a few dogs in those cabin days, including a unique black-and-white Harlequin Great Dane that I raised from a puppy. His name was Eric, and he was my sensitive, caring friend. We three loved that dog. He went everywhere with us, his big ol' head hanging out the van window.

Often, we drove a few hours away to Branson, Missouri, for music festivals, and we always took Eric along. Before the TV show *Hee Haw* had a theater that put Branson on the map, the music scene there was mostly a bunch of hippies who jammed and played bluegrass music in the town square. That's how the Branson phenomenon began. People like us went there to enjoy music and hang out with other hippies. Eric, who was quite the charmer, fit right in, and people lined up to pet him!

On one occasion, when we returned to the cabin after being in Branson for a festival, I immediately let the dogs out so they could run around. That included Eric, who'd been in the van for a couple of hours. Then Kim, Rhonda, and I decided to drive into Cape Girardeau for groceries.

When we got back a short time later, I called the dogs. They came in but seemed unsettled, and I realized Eric wasn't with them. Kim, Rhonda, and I kept calling him, but he never responded. I said, "Man, that's really strange. He always comes when we call him." Kim and I hopped back in the van and looked for Eric.

The area surrounding the cabin was full of good ol' farmers who were always nice to me. But hippies were a new thing back then, and a lot of folks didn't know what to make of us. One of the farmers was the local bully, and he outright disliked me because I was a hippie. The truth was, he hated everybody.

As we drove down the dirt road, I saw the bully farmer, his wife, and his kids outside. I pulled into his driveway and asked, "Hey, I don't mean to bother you, but you know my Great Dane?"

He said, "Yeah, I know."

"I can't find him," I explained. "Have you seen him?"

"Yeah, I shot him," he replied. "He was on my property."

Thinking he was lying about shooting my dog, I said, "Yeah, well, OK. Where is he?" I figured the guy had Eric tied up somewhere.

"He's down by the pond."

I walked over to the pond, which was about fifty yards away. The bully wasn't lying. Eric was lying there with a hole blown through him. Blood was everywhere, and flies were all over my dog's body.

I lost it. Rage filled me, and I decided that this was the last straw—I was going to kill him. As I stomped toward the bully, I thought, "I'll be in prison for the rest of my life, but I don't care. I'm just tired. I'm worn out. I'm tired of the drugs. I'm tired of the police. I'm going to kill this guy, and it'll be outright murder. I'll be locked up for the rest of my life, but it doesn't matter."

The thought of murdering Eric's killer contradicted everything I claimed to want at that time, which was to get past the violence through transcendental meditation and a vegetarian diet. I did drugs to calm myself down; I did peaceful things like making my own bread and churning my own butter, yet my rage returned in an instant.

Kim and the bully's wife were turned away from me, but the bully saw the violence on my face and backed up against the barn.

When I approached the guy to grab him, his wife screamed, "No!"

I tried reaching for him, but I couldn't lift my arms. I kept trying, but my arms would not move. I believe that God pinned down my arms to keep me from killing the man. All the while, his kids cried in terror as his wife begged, "Don't kill him! Don't kill him!"

I yelled back, "I'm going to kill him!" But I still couldn't lift my arms. I struggled and hollered, "God, let me go. Please let me go!"

Crying and screaming, Kim begged me, "Larry, don't. Please don't."

Nobody physically restrained me. Nothing visible pinned my arms to my sides. Only God stood between me and the man I wanted to murder. As the women screamed and sobbed, the man saw that I was insane with rage. All he could do was beg me for his life, screaming, "I'm sorry! I'm sorry!"

Physically unable to hurt the man, I started walking away. I told Kim, "Get the van and meet me back at the cabin. I'm going to carry Eric through the field and the woods." Then I looked at Eric's killer and said, "I'm coming back, and I'll kill you and everything you have."

I returned to the pond, ripped off my shirt, and picked up my Great Dane. I climbed over the barbed wire fence, tromped through the woods, and got back to my place with my huge dog in my arms and blood all over me.

Kim sat on the porch crying as I laid Eric down near the cabin, got a shovel, and dug him a grave. The whole time, I thought, "I will kill that guy. I'm going to murder him. As soon as I'm done burying Eric, I'm going back for that guy."

While I was still digging and Kim sat on the porch, a highway patrol car pulled up. Two state troopers got out and walked toward me. Eric's blood was smeared all over me, and Eric was still lying there. I glared at the troopers, and they stopped, turned, and approached Kim. "Can we talk to him?" they asked.

"I wouldn't right now if I were you," she said. "I'd wait a while."

I continued digging as they stood in the background, patiently waiting. Finally, I lowered Eric into the hole and covered him up. After fifteen minutes or so, they asked, "Larry, can we talk to you for a second?"

"You tell him I'm going to come back and kill everything he's got!" I fumed. "I'll kill everything."

"Look, we know who this guy is. We know what he's like," they responded. "But you can't take the law into your own hands."

"You just tell him, one night I'm coming back, and I'll kill everything."

They said, "You need to cool off, Larry. Don't do something you'll regret." Then they got in their car and drove off.

"Go to Flagstaff"

My rage boiled over, but just as I knew that God saved my life when I overdosed in Colombia, I knew He pinned down my arms and kept me from killing the bully. Deep down, I knew the troopers were right. I really didn't want to kill someone and be imprisoned for life. And with my track record, that was likely to happen sooner or later.

More than ever, I was determined to find God and get free. I received an invitation to study directly under the Maharishi Mahesh Yogi and was about to go when I came across a book called *Black Elk Speaks*.[1] It was popular with hippies and was about a Native American named Black Elk who found God on a mountaintop in the San Francisco Peaks outside Flagstaff, Arizona. When I read that, I sensed a prompt from something inside me: "Go to Flagstaff. You'll find God there." I knew the thought wasn't coming from me, and as bizarre as it sounds, I knew I had to go to Flagstaff.

About that time things started stirring again with the cops. So I told Kim and Rhonda, "Listen, I've got to get out of town."

They said, "Well, we want to get out too."

"I believe it's time for me to find God," I told them, "but I think it's going to be in Arizona."

They responded, "I guess we're moving to Arizona, then. Let's get out of here!"

That's what hippies did in those days. Among the three of us, we had some money to get to Flagstaff and get settled, but I sold my Harley—not only to have a financial cushion but also to secretly fund some drug selling here and there.

Chapter 6

PLEASE DON'T
LEAVE ME HERE

O
UR MINDS WERE made up. We were off to Flagstaff, and I was going to find God. But things played out differently from what any of us expected. Little did I know that the Holy Spirit had set me up. Kim, Rhonda, and I packed our stuff, tossed it in the VW van, and hit the road. With beads hanging from the rearview mirror and peace signs and flowers doodled everywhere, we were free-spirited hippies looking for purpose, meaning, and the promised land.

Not Lost Forever

In reality we were lost and wandering in the wilderness. About thirty miles into our trip we visited a friend of mine who was also a drug dealer. He had just acquired some heavy-duty hallucinogens and said, "Why don't you spend the night? We'll get high, and you can leave in the morning."

That sounded like a sweet offer, so we took him up on it and looked forward to getting high. My user friends had tagged me with the nickname OD (for "overdose") because if everybody took one tab of acid, I took three, with no questions asked. You would think I'd learned my lesson by then, but I hadn't. I took three hits of the hallucinogenic acid and went on a twenty-four-hour psychedelic trip. I was so out of it that we had to stay with my friend for an extra day. Neither he nor Kim and Rhonda thought I'd ever come out of it. Eventually I did, but my system needed some time to readjust before we could get back on the road.

As we drove toward Arizona, Kim looked at me with curiosity. "What were you seeing?" she asked.

"When?"

"You know, when you were tripping out."

Instead of answering, I gripped the steering wheel tightly and gazed straight ahead, my eyes focused on the road.

Kim continued, "You were under the kitchen table, and you kept screaming, 'God, don't leave me here! Oh my God, I'm lost forever. Don't leave me here!' Do you have any memory of that?"

"Yeah, yeah, I remember," I said. "I was trying to forget about it."

"You were holding onto the table legs for dear life, screaming, but what were you seeing?"

"I don't want to talk about it."

"Maybe you need to."

"It was the strangest thing," I replied. "I was in a black cubicle-like space in the middle of a vast, burning desert that stretched as far as I could see. I was trapped and kept asking God to help me get out. Then my perspective changed, and I was on a hill, looking down at myself in the same desert, trapped in the same black cubicle space. On the hill I was standing next to God. I wasn't looking at Him, but I could see Him from the corner of my eye. Something kept me from turning fully, but I knew it was Him. We were both looking down at the other me, who was below us, screaming, 'Please don't leave me here!' And I said to God, 'Why don't You help him?' And God answered, 'I wanted to, but now it's too late. He's lost forever.'"

As Kim's facial expression switched from inquisitive to distraught, I said, "Isn't that wild?"

I must have smirked, because she said, "That's not even funny."

"No, no," I said, "I don't think it's funny. I don't know what it is."

Remember that I had no Bible or church background other than what I've already mentioned. Neither did Rhonda. But Kim was a Pentecostal backslider. She didn't know it, but she had a well of Bible knowledge inside her, and it would bubble to the surface every now and then. The truth was that I didn't believe in hell or anything like that. Really, I didn't know anything.

Rhonda had sat quietly, taking in the conversation between Kim and me. Now all three of us became silent, lost in our own thoughts. The only sound in the van came from the staticky AM radio. As the wind whipped through our hair, Stephen Stills and Eric Clapton–type music played, and I pondered everything, including Eric, whom we all missed very much.

New Home, New Hope

After twenty-one hours of driving, we made it to Flagstaff, weary, worn, and looking for a place to put down roots. The van was home until we found a small, shabby unfurnished rental house. We tossed our bags and some mattresses on the floor, and we were set. The house was in the red-light district, among local bars and all the features that come with them. Locals would enter the bars, get drunk, and pass out on the sidewalks while women of the night plied their trade.

Looking back, I am certain that the Lord orchestrated our Flagstaff move—not just for me but for all three of us. I believe it was an answer to the prayer I prayed in Colombia: "God, don't let me die until I find what happiness is." What appeared to be a random series of terrible situations was actually an arrangement of stepping stones. God moved us to Arizona where I would experience an unforgettable encounter.

One night, while Kim and Rhonda took the van to run errands, I sat on the porch smoking a joint. Across the street I noticed a Hispanic guy in his late teens or early twenties walking along the sidewalk. It was apparent that he was a street kid. He glanced over at me and stepped to the curb to come my way. Then he stopped, appearing to pause and think things through.

After a moment the young man turned around and walked past again, watching me out of the corner of his eye. I assumed he was mustering up the nerve to ask whether I had any drugs to sell. He paced back and forth four or five times, and when he reached the end of the block again, he took a deep breath. Then he turned around, crossed the road, and walked up to me. I could tell he was nervous.

"I've never done this before," he said.

"You never bought dope before?" I replied.

"No. Not that," he said. "I don't want any drugs. I just couldn't walk away until I told you that Jesus is who you're looking for."

That was the third time I was told almost those exact words. And still, I didn't get it. "What did you say?" I asked, both shocked and annoyed.

"All I can tell you, man, is that I was a drug addict and some guys right down the street told me about Jesus. They put me in the back of a van and prayed with me." He continued, "I was so addicted that when I didn't have money for drugs, I would spray some paint in a rag and sniff the fumes. But when I asked Jesus into my heart, I got free. I'm free!"

Then he looked into my eyes and said, "I just couldn't walk away until I told you what He did for me and what He can do for you."

"OK," I responded, "you told me. Now get out of here. Go away."

"I'm telling you, it's real," he said. "Jesus is real."

When Kim and Rhonda came home, I told them about this crazy young guy who crossed the street to tell me about Jesus. As we talked, we heard a knock on the door. I peeked through the curtains. "It's him again," I said.

"Well, let him in," said Kim, the backslider.

So I opened the door for him. There were a couple of bags of weed around, and I was rolling joints. But our visitor didn't show the slightest interest in the drugs. He just started telling us how much Jesus loved us. When I mocked him, sadness came over his face, and he turned to leave. "Listen," he said, pausing at the door, "why don't you guys come to church with me?"

"Yeah, well, that ain't going to happen," I snapped.

"You should think about it," he said.

I assured him, "Nope. Not going to happen."

The Gospel on Film

The young man's name was Bill Trujillo. He left quietly that evening, but he kept showing up over the next few weeks. When we saw him coming, we tried to ignore him. Yet because we had no furniture, we sat on the mattress, which was on the floor. He'd knock and say, "I know you're there. I saw you."

Each time, we opened the door, and he told us the same thing: "Jesus is what you're looking for."

I always shut him down and said, "Bye." But he just kept coming over.

One night he said, "Listen, we're showing a movie called *The Gospel Road* at church this Friday. Why don't you come check it out?"

This time I said, "OK, I'll go to the movie with you if you promise to quit bugging us about this Jesus stuff."

"Just come to the movie," he insisted.

"We'll be there," I said. "Then you can leave us alone."

Rhonda and I went to see the film. Kim couldn't go because she'd gotten a job as a private night nurse caring for a man who had cancer. After dropping her off, we headed to the church, a little wooden building that seemed full with maybe sixty or seventy people inside. Most of them looked like regular church folks to me, but there were some young people sprinkled in.

Johnny Cash narrated the movie, wrote some of the soundtrack, and performed on some of the songs. June Carter played the role of Mary Magdalene and contributed to the soundtrack, as did Kris Kristofferson.[1] I was already a big fan of all three artists, so that got my attention.

The film depicted Jesus and the disciples as almost hippie-like characters, which also got my attention. As the ending unfolded, I saw the dramatic scene of Jesus hanging on the cross at Calvary and, of course, dying. Then the scene changed, and Jesus was hanging on the cross in Times Square, with street people like me all around Him. Once again, His head dropped, and He died. Then the scene jumped again to Jesus dying on the cross in the streets of East Los Angeles.

The shifting locations punched me in the gut. I realized that Jesus didn't die only for church people. He died for us street people. That movie and its music began the soundtrack for my life and fifty years of serving God! Music is so powerful and able to penetrate hearts and minds like nothing else can. It certainly penetrated mine that evening.

May God keep on using music through today's generation and future generations to touch souls, break down walls, melt hearts, and transform lives in supernatural ways!

Somebody Touched Me

Though the church that ran *The Gospel Road* was housed in an old building, it was a new church plant. The young pastor, Ron Burrell, had been the lead singer and guitar player in a rock group called Eden, from Prescott, Arizona. Eden was the backup group for some leading rock and roll bands. They were in the process of signing a contract with Elektra Records when Ron suddenly gave his life to the Lord. The other band members eventually did the same, and their wild rock group transformed into a gospel rock and roll band. This caused a chain reaction, with hundreds of young people in the area deciding to follow the Lord. The Jesus movement had come to Arizona.

The Jesus movement became so widespread that *Time* magazine devoted cover stories in 1971 and 1972 to its impact on America.[2] Parts of the free-spirited hippie movement morphed into the Jesus movement, and it swept through Prescott. The new wave of Christian music served as a bridge to reach the younger generation. Eden's members became part of the town's Foursquare church and started a major youth movement there.

Now Ron had brought the fire of the Jesus movement with him to pioneer this church in Flagstaff. After the movie, Pastor Ron gave an altar call, saying, "If you want to give your life to the Lord, come forward." I had just realized that Jesus died for people like me, but I was not about to go forward in front of everyone! Nobody had greeted Rhonda and me or even made eye contact with us. Maybe it was the Colombian poncho I was wearing or the fact that I wore no shirt underneath it. I could be rather intimidating, with rings on every finger, bare feet, and needle marks up and down my arms, not to mention my long hair, the bags under my eyes, and my feather earrings.

Although that congregation would become my church and many of those people would become my friends, they didn't know what to do with Rhonda and me that night. Looking back, I realize that it was a case of what 1 Samuel 16:7 describes: Man looks on the outside, but God looks on the inside. Rhonda and I needed Jesus, but we didn't quite fit in.

Is that why I held off going forward? Maybe partly. I fiercely resisted the altar call, but the pebbles in my shoe kept nudging me. So I watched as a few people went forward. Then Rhonda leaned over and whispered, "What do you think?"

I just shrugged. The two of us were glued to our seats, not moving, but Pastor Ron kept saying, "I feel like there's somebody else. I just feel like there's somebody else."

To this day, I don't remember getting out of my seat and walking to the front, yet suddenly Rhonda and I were kneeling at that altar. It had to be God, because there we were, on our knees! Personally, I had no understanding of heaven, hell, or being born again. And I certainly didn't know what to do. However, there was something about seeing Jesus die on the streets that bypassed my understanding and went directly into my soul. In that moment, I knew that He was what I was looking for.

People gathered around and prayed for all the others who had come forward, but nobody prayed with Rhonda and me. I realized that I still seemed intimidating to the people in the church, so they kept their distance. Only Bill Trujillo and Pastor Ron seemed unaffected by my appearance.

Undeterred by the distance I felt from the congregation, I said, "God, if You're real, be real to me." When the words came out, I instantly felt as though a million pounds lifted off my shoulders. I began to weep, crying real tears for the first time since the day my dad tried to give me away. What happened at that altar was a totally new experience. I had no idea what it was or what to call it. But like Bill Trujillo and my former college teammate had said, it was real.

While tears streamed down my face, Pastor Ron put his hand on my shoulder. "God really touched you, didn't He, son?"

I pushed his hand away and said, "Well, somebody did."

When the altar call was done, everybody went back to their seats. Still, nobody engaged with us except Pastor Ron and Bill. That was partly my fault. I didn't trust anybody and showed a hard exterior that kept some people away.

Later in the van, Rhonda, who had also given her life to the Lord, asked (as if I knew the answer), "What was that?"

"Man, something powerful!"

We felt so good that we went and bought an expensive bag of dope and a bottle of whiskey to celebrate.

And still, God kept drawing us to Himself.

Chapter 7

WE GOT "BORNED AGAIN"

I T WAS WELL after midnight on July 5, 1975, when we picked up Kim from work. She got in the van, which was full of pot smoke, and asked, "What'd you guys do tonight?"

"You're not going to believe it," I answered. "We went to church."

Rhonda and I were all giggly and high.

Kim asked soberly, "What?"

"Yeah," I said, "we got borned again today."

We had no idea what that meant (or that we were mispronouncing it), but we were celebrating because we felt it. The term *born again* comes from Jesus' encounter with Nicodemus when He says, "Most assuredly, I say to you, unless one is born again, he cannot see the kingdom of God" (John 3:3). Once someone is born again, they are in Christ, and "if anyone is in Christ, he is a new creation; old things have passed away; behold, all things have become new" (2 Cor. 5:17).

The words *borned again* got Kim's attention. "You got what?" she asked.

I said, "Listen, Jesus died on the cross, and on the seventh day, He rose again. And by us asking Him to forgive us, we're borned again."

"What are you smoking?"

"Oh man," I said, "I called Mike, and we got some really good stuff."

"You're not born again," Kim said.

"No, no, no, you don't understand," I explained. "He died and He was dead for seven days. And on the seventh day, I don't know, He ended up in heaven or something."

"No, you guys aren't born again," she repeated.

And Rhonda insisted, "Yes, we are."

What Kim didn't tell us was that she had received a letter from her mom that day. In it, her mom said, "Kim, God spoke to my heart and said something's going to happen to Larry real soon, and it's going to open the door for you to come back to the Lord. It's your time to turn your life and lifestyle around."

Digging in My Heels

Even though we'd been "borned again," I didn't want to go back to that church. When Kim and Rhonda said they wanted to go, I protested, saying, "I'm not going. Those people are downright unfriendly."

Later that week, however, I came home from being out, and Kim and Rhonda said, "You know that preacher from the church?"

"Yeah."

"Well, he came by. Bill Trujillo told him where we lived."

"What did he want?" I asked.

"Well," said Kim, "he wanted to know if we needed any money for groceries."

"You didn't take it, did you?"

"No. We knew you'd be furious if we did."

"We don't need help from nobody," I barked.

"But he seemed like a really nice guy."

"No," I said. "We don't need anything."

The next day, believe it or not, some Baha'i people knocked on our door and invited us to one of their meetings. Unlike the church people, they were extremely friendly and warm. So instead of going to church, Rhonda and I went to a Baha'i meeting. (Kim was working again.) It was interesting, and as we walked to the van afterward, I asked Rhonda, "What did you think?"

She just shrugged.

"They're a lot friendlier than those church people were," I noted. "But I didn't feel here what I felt there."

"Yeah," she said, "me either."

Like me, Rhonda had no religious background, but because of the letter Kim had received from her mom, both women decided, "We're going to go to church this Sunday."

I was unconvinced and unwilling to follow their lead. "Not me," I told them, digging in my heels. "I'm not going."

Over the next few weeks, Kim and Rhonda attended church a couple of times. When they did, I promptly mocked them and said stuff like, "Did you lift your hands and shout 'Hallelujah'?"

One of them said, "So what if we did, Larry? It's OK, you know."

"I'll never do it," I said.

Knocked Off the Fence

Although I was born again, I was also dealing drugs here and there and getting a little too much attention from the police. So we moved to some cabins out in the woods—kind of a hippie commune type of thing. Each cabin had electricity, but there was a communal shower and toilet.

One day, Kim and Rhonda said, "Hey, this guy from Phoenix is coming to preach. They say he's something else. Why don't you come see him with us?"

For some reason, I said, "OK, I'll go."

The preacher's name was John Metzler, and he was going to hold revival-type services at Ron Burrell's church for a whole week. He moved in the gifts of the Spirit, giving words of wisdom and words of knowledge. I'd never seen anything like that. It was amazing, but it freaked me out a little.

The man himself freaked me out too. He was the polar opposite of me. He had coiffed hair and wore a suit and tie, French cuffs, and shiny shoes—a total contrast to my junkie-hippie look. I thought, "I don't belong in a place like this. Look at how this guy's dressed."

Reverend Metzler also made a comment right off the bat that ruffled my feathers. He called me out and spoke to me during the altar call at the end of the service. I realized later that he was making an effort to relate to people like me, but I got defensive. He said, "I can remember when Ron Burrell first got saved. He had such long hair, he looked like an orangutan." I eventually understood that he wasn't making fun of those of us with long hair. But in the moment, I took it that way, and I immediately shut down.

Rhonda knew that something had gotten under my skin. She started praying, "God, if You don't do something, if You don't touch Larry, he'll never come back. It'll be over."

Rhonda read me right. I just glared at this preacher, thinking, "How dare you insult me."

Later, John and I became dear friends, but in those first moments, I was too angry to hear a word he said. Then he started ministering to people. He called up one lady and said, "You went to the doctor on Tuesday, and he said such and such about you."

The woman said, "Yeah, that's right."

John laid hands on her, and she dropped to the floor. I now recognize this as being slain in the Spirit, but back then, I'd never seen anything like it. I thought, "What in the world? Did he knock that lady down? What did he do?"

While John ministered and everybody else praised God, I got angrier. I looked at Kim and Rhonda, but they were both praying intently. They'd been going to church almost nightly for a couple of weeks and were seriously into it. Meanwhile, I was still getting high and was not quite into what God was doing.

As John prophesied and the people continued praising God, I thought, "I hate this. I'll never come back here. This is the most foolish thing I've ever seen." Yet I couldn't deny that something was stirring within my heart.

Soon, John said, "Let's just all praise God," and the whole congregation (including Kim and Rhonda) stood and lifted their hands. This was nothing new to Kim. She was raised Pentecostal and was Spirit-filled, so she was returning to her spiritual roots. And Rhonda didn't seem to mind at all. But my flesh was in an uproar. None of what I saw made any sense. Still, I felt something.

Sitting down with my eyes closed and my hands lifted only as high as my stomach, I muttered, mostly to myself, "God, if this is real, let me know. Let me know if this is real."

I thought nobody could see me, but I felt someone touch my fingers. When I opened my eyes, I saw John Metzler looking right at me. "Son," he said, "come here. God's got a word for you."

You have to picture the scene and remember that John was talking to a stone-cold junkie with obvious needle marks and big, black bags under his eyes. Yet he said, "Come here. God wants to touch you."

I was sitting next to the aisle in the second row—the same place I sat every time I attended that church. John stood me up in the aisle and said, "You were just speaking to God."

I wanted to say, "OK, yeah. Well, maybe my lips were moving," but I never got the words out.

"You just said to God, 'Lord, if this is real, let me know. Let me know if this is real.'"

That was exactly what I had prayed. "Wow!" I thought. Then I reasoned, "Well, maybe that's a common thing that people pray."

"You want everything God has to offer, don't you?" he asked.

I looked him square in the eye and said, "Yeah, if it comes from God and not you."

He just smiled and said, "Receive it."

He put his hand on my forehead as Pastor Ron stood behind me. I had just seen people slain in the Spirit and thought, "I'm definitely not playing that game." But when John touched me, I experienced something like slow motion. Everybody said I shot back so fast that Pastor Ron missed catching me. But I felt like I was floating.

When I came to, I was flat on my back, speaking in tongues— me, the guy who mocked Kim and Rhonda about lifting their hands and shouting "Hallelujah!" and who swore that I would *never* do something like that.

Years later, Tiz and I pastored among the Navajo and learned a Navajo proverb that essentially says, "When you mock something, you're the next one to do it." Maybe I hadn't yelled "Hallelujah!" yet, but I was on my back, praying in tongues with Pastor Ron straddling me and some older

African American church ladies with big hats laying hands on me! I didn't want to do it, but I couldn't stop.

As I lay there, John kept praying out loud, "Lord, don't let him up until he knows it's You. Don't let him up."

I was frozen in place.

Listen, I hate when people fake the Holy Spirit. That kind of show, as well as everything that goes with it, repulses me. I tell people that the baptism in the Holy Spirit normally doesn't happen the way it happened to me. But I really believe God knew that if I walked out that night without being filled by Him, I would never come back.

"This Is the Night"

The congregation went on having church while I lay sprawled on the floor, embarrassed and humiliated and speaking in tongues. Finally, I gathered enough strength to get up on my knees and crawl to my seat. When I got there, Rhonda asked, "What the heck was that?"

I answered her question with one of my own. "What did that guy do to me? *What* did he do to me?"

"I don't know," she said.

All I knew was that something big had happened. Part of my morning routine was to roll a pack of joints with a cigarette-rolling machine and carry the pack all day. On the morning after this experience at church, I started rolling a joint and stopped. I told Kim and Rhonda, "You know what? I'm not going to smoke today."

Flabbergasted, they asked, "Why not?"

"Man, I'm still high from last night." I was speaking about being so deeply touched by the Holy Spirit.

You know, on the day of Pentecost, the onlookers accused

those who were filled with the Spirit of being drunk. And Peter said, we "are not drunk, as you suppose" (Acts 2:15). He didn't say, "We aren't drunk." He essentially said, "We aren't drunk the way you think. But we are drunk in the Holy Ghost. We're filled with God's Spirit."

I didn't know about all that at the time, but I told Kim and Rhonda, "I don't want to come down from this high, and I don't want to smoke this joint."

They were getting ready for the day and didn't say much. But they asked me whether I was planning to go to church that night. "Yeah, I'm going," I answered. "I want to watch that guy again."

So we all went to church, and at the end of the service, John started ministering to people again. Even after all that happened the night before, I repeated the same prayer: "God, let me know if this is real." And just like the night before, I kept my eyes closed and my hands partially raised. Then I felt John touching my fingers, and I opened my eyes.

"Son," he said, "God's got a word for you. This is the night." Then he said it again: "God's got a word for you."

"OK," I mumbled.

As I stood there, he continued, "You're going to preach the gospel around the world. God's going to use you in ways that will astound you."

"What?" I thought. "This guy's an idiot. I'm not even coming back here tomorrow, and he's telling me I'm going to be a preacher."

John said, "God wants to touch you," and he put his hand on me. *Boom!*—I dropped to the floor again and lay there speaking in tongues, embarrassed but unable to stop.

The next night, Kim, Rhonda, and I all returned to church.

For the third time, John had a word for me: "You're going to be used. You're going to write books and do many things."

My mind was blown. "Look at me," I thought. On the one hand, I was resisting God, but on the other, I was leaning forward, not wanting to go backward. And down I went, flat on my back for the third night in a row!

On the way home that night, I asked Kim and Rhonda, "How does this guy do it?"

"That's the Holy Spirit," said Kim.

"No," I said. "He's shocking me somehow."

"It's the Holy Spirit," she repeated.

I told myself, "OK, I'll go back one more time."

On the fourth night, I sat on my seat and prayed, "God, if this is real, don't let him knock me on my back. If it's really You and not some trick or some kind of witchcraft, don't let him knock me on my back. Then I'll know it's real."

Once again, John prophesied to me and told me things that God was going to do. When he went to lay his hands on me, I prayed silently, "Don't let him knock me on my back and I'll know it's You." Then my feet shot out from under me, and I fell forward, onto my knees at the altar. But John never touched me. He simply raised his hands, and down I went.

All I could do was put my elbows on the altar and tell the Lord, "I'm going to serve You for the rest of my life."

That was the beginning of a whole new life. I got involved with the church and with being discipled. I was amazed at how fast the news spread. Some of my friends from St. Louis and Cape Girardeau heard what happened in Arizona. They heard our church was doing a lot of mission work in Mexico, so they figured, "Larry Huch in church? Sure. Mission work in Mexico? Yeah, right. He's going in with the church and smuggling drugs back to the States."

Of course, what they said was ridiculous and was based on my past. They simply didn't know the new me.

———•———

Before my encounters with the Holy Spirit, I continued mainlining cocaine, but I used less because I was short on cash. I used anything I could afford, including acid, psilocybin mushrooms, and marijuana. Kim and Rhonda didn't like stuff being around the house, so I had to hide it from them.

My experience with the Holy Spirit baptism helps me grasp Jesus' last instruction to His disciples. Before He ascended, He said, "Don't leave without the Holy Spirit." (See Luke 24:49.) Here's why, in my experience: Although I had become a Christian, I wasn't delivered until I received the power of God through the Holy Spirit within me. Yes, I had already given my life to the Lord, but I received power when I was baptized in the Holy Spirit.

Since those nights when I was laid out and woke up speaking in tongues, I have never done drugs. Nothing! Think about it. For years, I was a junkie. I couldn't go an hour without some drug or other in my system. If something didn't change, I was going to either die or enter a serious rehab program. Yet when the Spirit touched me, I stopped cold turkey, without any withdrawal symptoms or cravings.

That is a miracle!

Chapter 8

EVERYBODY'S IN CHAINS BUT ME

For four nights in a row, John Metzler prophesied to me. I didn't look like someone who would preach the gospel, yet he told me I would preach around the world, become a pastor, write books, and do other godly things. On the fourth night, I realized that what happened was from God, and I decided, "You know what? I'm going to serve God for the rest of my life, and I'm going to give my life to telling people what Jesus has done for me."

I soon discovered that God's call didn't mean serving Him would be easy. Sometimes the greatest opposition comes from religious people. One Sunday I was in the church men's room washing my hands, and one of the elders was there. I looked in the mirror and saw him behind me, staring at me. When I turned around, he said, "God will never use you. God will never use you."

Mind you, he was an elder in the church, and I was a new convert. So I asked him, "Why won't God use me? Why won't He?"

"Because you laugh too much," he said dryly. "The gospel is serious."

I looked at him and answered, "You know what? I did enough crying in my beer before I knew Jesus. Now I'm going to rejoice in the Lord."

Testifying to Men in Chains

When I was at church the following Sunday, some of the men said, "Listen, on Sunday mornings, we go down to the jail and witness to the inmates. Why don't you come with us?"

I thought, "I don't know any Bible, but OK."

That Sunday we went to the jail in Flagstaff—just two guys from the church and me. When we arrived, the guard pointed and said, "We've got two drunk tanks: one over here and one over there. And then down that corridor, we have a room for dangerous felons who are waiting for transport to the penitentiary."

Guess what happened? Each of the men who invited me took one of the drunk tanks, and they sent me to minister to the dangerous felons. I walked into a crowded room where twenty-five or thirty men in orange jumpsuits were chained in their seats. Everybody was in chains but me.

The guard told me, "Stand right here next to the door. If anything goes wrong, push this buzzer, and we'll come as soon as we can."

I was only a few weeks old in the Lord and knew almost nothing about the Bible. So I shared my testimony about how Jesus set me free. When I was finished, every man in the room gave his life to the Lord. That's not an exaggeration. When the guards and the church men came to get us, I and all the chained men were kneeling on the floor, praying together to accept the Lord. I knew that, just as God had honored my prayers when I knew nothing, He would honor theirs.

This experience reminds me of a time when the Trinity Broadcasting Network asked Mike Barber and me to hold a service at Angola, an infamous prison in Louisiana, because the warden's dad had heard my testimony. Angola is an unbelievably violent place. At one point in time, only 15 percent of Angola's prisoners would ever make it out. Eighty-five percent never would, serving life sentences.[1]

The meeting was held outdoors, and guards with large guns were posted all around the walls and on the towers. White, black, and brown men sat and listened to my testimony. I told them that getting delivered from drugs wasn't the hard part for me; my biggest struggle was with anger and violence. I told them how my dad was a violent guy and how his dad was a violent guy. I shared about breaking family and generational curses. Later I found out that's why they wanted me to come.

At the end of my message, I asked the men, "How many of you have a father or grandfather in prison?"

Almost every hand shot up.

"How many of you have a son or grandson in prison?"

Again, almost every man raised a hand. It was staggering.

"Well, let's break these family curses," I said. "Let's break these generational curses, and let's start with breaking the curses of anger and racism—the 'I don't like you because you're white, you're black, you're brown' curse. Let's break them all." I continued, "If you're ready to break these family curses, I want you to come forward and pray with me."

I didn't know that the men had been instructed not to move from their chairs, stand up, or even sneeze. But God moved so strongly on breaking these curses that most of the men got up and came to kneel at the front. When they first stood up, the guards freaked out. Then the warden said, "It's OK," and we all knelt together.

Men of every color and kindred ended up hugging one another because they understood that Jesus would do more than forgive sin—He would gladly break the iniquity that causes sin. Iniquities are the driving force that triggers people to act in certain sinful ways. That is a big part of what we have learned with breaking generational curses: What is passed on is not just the sin or the act but the driving force inside that causes human beings to stumble.

The following week, the prison chaplain called and said, "Pastor, I just want you to know that of all the meetings we have held here and all the pastors who have come in and taught and preached, what we're seeing since your meeting is the most tangible change we have ever witnessed in the inmates here. Here it is, a week later, and we can still sense the difference in these men."

What we shared with the inmates wasn't just an encouraging word but a lasting transformation from the Holy Spirit. It was tangible proof of the power of God to break curses. To this day, we consistently receive letters from prisoners across the country and around the world.

The Flagstaff jail was my first ministry. Back in those hippie days, a group from the church and I also did a lot of street ministry. I can remember witnessing in the red-light district where all the bars and prostitutes were—the area where Kim, Rhonda, and I once lived. An intimidating, rough-looking, six-foot-four or six-foot-five guy named Lucky was the main overseer of all the working girls. One night, we were still preaching and sharing individually when Lucky walked up to us. As we talked with him, he kept looking at me. Then, when everybody else walked away, he asked me, "What are you on, man?"

I said, "What?"

He pressed, "Come on, man. Your eyes are too bright. What are you on?"

I finally convinced him that it was the Holy Spirit, the presence of Jesus. Wouldn't you know, he showed up at church the following Sunday with his eight-year-old son, and Lucky gave his life to Jesus!

The ministry didn't stop there. The group that we led to the Lord on those streets began sharing with others and leading them to the Lord. It was a domino effect. We did everything we could to evangelize and raise young men and women who would go into the ministry. So in Flagstaff I worked to become grounded in the Scripture and in church, and I became the leader of our church's coffeehouse.

As I said earlier, rock and folk-type music played a significant role in the Jesus movement. Christian coffeehouses popped up all across the country, and the Jesus movement ultimately birthed contemporary Christian music. Our church in Flagstaff tapped into all that. We threw together little bands and groups and often turned worldly songs into Jesus songs. We called it "getting a song saved." "Jesus Is Just Alright," recorded by the secular group The Doobie Brothers, reached number 35 on the secular charts in February 1973,[2] showing the impact that the Jesus movement had on the larger culture. Our coffeehouse was a cool place for both Jesus people and searching souls to hang out. Although the Holy Spirit brought conviction, there was no judgment, and Jesus met us there.

Ministering in the streets by talking and praying with real people was preparation for our lives as pastors. The streets were our training ground, and the coffeehouse was where we learned how to relate to people, counsel with them, preach, share our testimonies, and minister to them. With no official training in the Scriptures, our group learned by soaking up the Word and walking hand in hand with people wherever they were. My formal Bible and spiritual training would come in due season, but our foundation was birthed in and built on our love for God and His people, our compassion for all, and our dedication to one-on-one, boots-on-the-ground work.

My personal freedom from drugs, violence, and anger did not come through counseling or rehab. It evolved as I poured my life into serving God and helping others. There's nothing wrong with counseling or rehab, but moving forward and bringing healing to the hurting are the things that brought healing to me. My passion for sin turned into a passion for God and for knowing Him. My addiction to drugs, alcohol, and sin evolved into an addiction to God, His Word, and His presence. My desire to use drugs transformed into a desire to be used by God. Whatever He had done for me, I would spend my life helping others know that He wanted to do it for them too.

Although breaking free from my anger took time, it happened. God channeled that anger into a righteous indignation at what the world and the enemy were doing to destroy people's lives. My inner drive for adventures and my disposition as an adrenaline junkie became a drive for experiencing God's presence and miracles. I had long been consumed with sin; now I was consumed with Him. I didn't set out to become a Bible scholar. I didn't intend to fill my mind with biblical or religious facts. I wanted (and still want) only a heart for God and His reality.

The only thing I knew as a brand-new Christian was that Jesus had touched me and set me free. I didn't know the answers to people's questions. I knew only what I had experienced in God. Salvation changed me (as it changes all of us) from the inside out. It gave me a whole new set of desires so that everything I craved revolved around God. My faith was raw, and it was real.

It has been fifty years since the Lord came into my life and rescued me. But with Jesus, the story never ends. I'm more excited about God and His Word today than I was on day one of being saved. It truly is "exceedingly abundantly above all that [I could] ask or think" (Eph. 3:20). From the beginning, I knew what God had saved me *from*, but I began a journey of finding out what He saved me *for*. I discovered what He longed to do *for* me and *through* me.

What I've learned has been transformative. God took this worldly thrill seeker and made me a godly thrill seeker. In my quest to find peace, I found the Peacemaker. In my quest for the next high, I found the highest high. And in my quest to find love, I found the greatest love the world has ever known.

Only God could do all that. Only He could make me free.

Chapter 9

AN UNEXPECTED ADVENTURE

Once the Holy Spirit moved inside me, He immediately shifted the "furniture" of my life and even tossed some of it out. That's what He does. The Holy Spirit never leaves us as we are. The moment we are born again, the process of making us more like Jesus begins. It's impossible to remain unchanged with the Holy Spirit inside you. If there is no change, let me challenge you to press in to the Holy Spirit a little bit more. Let Him change you from glory to glory, taking your life to new and better levels. (See 2 Corinthians 3:18.)

The apostle Paul wrote, "Therefore, if anyone is in Christ, he is a new creation; old things have passed away; behold, all things have become new" (2 Cor. 5:17). While the change in the inner person is real and instant, transformation of the outer person usually takes time. Some issues and sinful patterns take longer to resolve than others. Chains that bind can be snapped instantly, bringing immediate freedom. That's called a miracle. But the Lord breaks other chains by gradually filing them down until they give way and fall off. That's a miracle too. In the process we learn to trust His presence and promises.

When I was first born again, I was still a junkie with a brain fried by drugs. But after I encountered the power of the Holy Spirit during those revival nights with John Metzler, the chains of addiction broke off miraculously. The Holy Spirit began not only restoring my mind but also doing so much more—now I had Him inside me to guide me.

Being conformed to the image of Christ is a lifetime process that will be completed only in His eternal presence. Meanwhile, God uses every circumstance—both good and bad—to mold us. To quote Romans 8:28 again, "All things work together for good to those who love God, to those who are the called according to His purpose."

When we are fully committed to loving and serving God, no matter what the world throws at us or what comes our way, God will take it and work it for the good in our lives. Tiz uses the illustration of a woven tapestry. Looking at the top side, it is a beautiful, intricate work of art. But if you look at the underside, it's a chaotic mess of light and dark colors that make no sense and seem completely random. Sometimes our lives appear from our perspective to be a random chaotic mess. But from God's perspective it is a beautifully woven tapestry made up of light and dark that creates an intricate work of art. God is a good God. He never causes bad things to happen in our lives, but He uses them to work His purposes, His goodness, His miracles, and His blessings in our lives.

Kim, Rhonda, and I had our individual, life-transforming experiences with the Lord, and each of us was molded by them. From the beginning, the Holy Spirit convicted Kim and me about living together. Knowing that our lifestyle was not pleasing to God, we separated but continued as friends, both attending our church in Flagstaff.

With the drugs gone, there was no question about whether Kim and I would lay down the immorality. God had answered my prayer and shown Himself to be real, and He wanted all of me. I became absorbed in the coffeehouse and street ministries while soaking up as much of the Bible as I could. Instead of selling drugs, I got a job in construction. Kim ended up marrying one of my good friends at the church, and they went into ministry. It was truly a God thing.

A New Chapter and New Life

I believed that I would get married too, but I figured it would happen way down the line. I had so much growing to do and so much that the Lord needed to heal. What I didn't expect was that the coolest, most beautiful young lady would enter the church doors and totally wreck me. Of course, I played it cool on the outside, but I was a mess on the inside!

It was more than Tiz's outward beauty; I felt drawn to her in a way I had never been drawn to anyone. Then, when she encountered the Lord in a life-altering way, our spirits began to mesh. God was bringing us together and would use us as a team to reach the world. All the romance was there, like it is for any young couple in love. Yet we sensed that something else was going on; something deeper was pulling us together.

Of course, there were kinks in our relationship that we needed to work out—mainly my rough edges and deep-seated anger issues. On so many occasions, God used Tiz to help smooth me out. It was all part of the growing process that transformed and prepared us for what God had in mind.

Together, we would become a force for God's kingdom. The Bible says that one can put a thousand to flight but two can put ten thousand to flight. (See Joshua 23:10 and Deuteronomy

32:30.) Those words could not be truer with Tiz and me. We had no idea of the extent to which the Lord would use us. We knew only that we were meant to be, and it was obviously a God thing, at least to us.

Although the Lord was in our relationship and our spirits meshed, we could not have been further apart in the natural. Tiz's family was right out of *Leave It to Beaver*, while mine was more like *Hill Street Blues*. My hometown of South St. Louis was full of poverty, bullets, drugs, and street fights. And as you know, my dad beat me and threw me out of the house. Tiz came from an entirely different world—from Helena, Montana. Her life was filled with skiing, hiking, cute cafés, a lakeside cabin, and postcards. Her parents adored her and were her best friends.

Tiz and I had some things in common, however: We each had our own kind of brokenness. I had been searching for peace and purpose by chasing the next drug high, money, immorality, and alternative sources of spirituality. Tiz searched too, but she tried all the good-life activities that a dream location could offer. I once looked like an all-American who had it all together but didn't. Tiz looked beautiful and almost perfect on the outside, yet she was also empty and lost.

So Tiz left the security of Montana to attend Northern Arizona University and expand herself. She got what she asked for—just not the way she envisioned. Her dorm roommate, whom she'd just met, invited her to church. Tiz was reluctant to go, but not knowing anyone else, she figured, "Why not?"

She had no idea what awaited her, but God did. Just as He had directed my steps since my first cries to Him in Colombia, He directed Tiz, who had cried out in her own way.

Listen as she tells her story.

Finding What Was Missing (Tiz)

My parents raised me with loose Christian principles, and we were not devoutly religious. On special occasions like Christmas and Easter, we attended the local Catholic church; then we resumed our secular lives. My upbringing was more focused on practical living than on God.

My parents were wonderful, wholesome people but were also very progressive and business-minded. My dad was a printer for the city newspaper. My mom was a legal secretary. They started their own business together combining legal secretarial and printing services. Neither of them was born into wealth, but they were hardworking, innovative people, pressing forward to build a better life.

In later years my mom became the executive administrator for a Montana senator. Being active in politics, my parents raised me to be involved as well. When I was a little girl, I'd go to their office on my bike after school and then deliver legal documents back and forth to the lawyers for whom my mom worked.

I learned a lot of valuable life principles from watching my parents. From an early age I was dialed into the legal, business, and political worlds. These influences modeled the core values in which my siblings and I were raised. We knew we could achieve whatever we wanted in life, but we knew we'd have to work for it, have integrity, and care about people. My parents had all those qualities, even though they didn't know the Lord or His power in a deeply personal way.

In high school I had an initial experience with the Lord, and seeds were planted. The Jesus movement came to Helena, and I attended a Bible study with a friend who'd just been born again. God really touched me that night, and I knew He was real. But since I didn't live it, it went no further. However, the seed was in my heart, and I knew there was something more about God.

Ours was a loving family in an amazing environment that some would consider a dream life. People came from everywhere to vacation at the place I called home. I was popular in school and active in sports, so I loved snow skiing in the winter and waterskiing in the summer. My parents built us a little cabin on a lake, and much of my growing up revolved around that lake—not only because of the waterskiing and water sports but also because of all the fun and family to enjoy.

Even though I always felt loved and had everything any young person could possibly want, something was missing from my life. I regularly asked myself, "Why do I feel so empty? I should be happy and content, but I feel like I'm missing something. Is this all there is to life?"

I was searching for something deeper. I knew that I'd had a great life in Montana. My family wasn't rich, but we were well off, thanks to a strong work ethic. So I felt guilty for feeling that what I had wasn't enough. I remember a song that Peggy Lee sang back in those days titled "Is That All There Is?"[1] It spoke to the emptiness in my soul, and I wondered what that emptiness was about. Today, I understand what C. S. Lewis said: "If I find in myself a desire which no experience in this world can satisfy, the most probable explanation is that I was made for another world."[2]

My questioning persisted, and during my second year at the University of Montana, I became unusually disillusioned and unsettled. I called my parents and said, "I'm dropping out of college for a while and going to live somewhere until I figure this thing out."

I couldn't decide whether I should go to Alaska to make

lots of money working on the pipeline, go to Aspen to become a ski bum, or travel overseas to experience another culture. Wherever it was, I wanted something different, and I believed an adventure was the answer. I didn't realize it, but my sense of being unsettled and disillusioned was part of God stirring my heart for more.

It so happened that at Christmastime a friend of mine came home from attending Northern Arizona University in Flagstaff. She told me she loved it, because Arizona was cool and many cool things were happening there. Plus, there was plenty of snow, as well as mountains and skiing opportunities. Something about what she said resonated with me, and I thought, "That sounds great!"

The next day, I called the university and filled out an application, and they accepted me. I packed my bags and skis, and off I went. I hadn't picked a full major; I just signed up for all kinds of classes—everything from the arts to environmental studies, from ecology to sociology. I wanted to help people and make a difference. Also, I believed that environmental studies and forestry would help save the planet.

I was all over the board, but I had a real passion for people and for life, and I longed to make a difference. Montana is one of the most beautiful places on the planet, and I wanted to protect and preserve that. But the Lord had something else in mind: He would use me to save souls instead of trees.

My parents scratched their heads at my choice to relocate and didn't like how far away I'd gone. They eventually warmed up to the idea and figured I'd be back once I got something out of my system and "found myself." I also think they were relieved to know that I wasn't dropping out of college altogether. So I arrived in Flagstaff looking for adventure—and, boy, did I find it, in the most unlikely place!

The Lord knows what our souls need, even when we don't. Soon after reaching the dorm and unpacking my stuff, I ended up not in the nearby mountains, trails, and places around town that I intended to visit but at the altar of a little church, crying my eyes out. I was there only because my new roommate asked me to go with her. I was like, "Church? Why would I go to church? I didn't come here for church."

"Just come with me and see what this is about," she answered. "I know the guy who's preaching."

"OK," I said. "Whatever!"

The church was small, seating about sixty people, and nearly every seat was taken. It was definitely not like the Catholic church I'd attended in Helena. It was also Pentecostal, which was a whole new experience for me. When things started getting loud and crazy, I thought, "I've got to get out of here! This is too weird."

As I planned my escape to the parking lot, someone gave an altar call. I sensed something tugging on my heart, and I burst into tears. Then I found myself going forward. It was the first time that I'd heard the pure gospel, and I knew instinctively that it was exactly what my soul was seeking. At the altar I asked the Lord into my heart, and an indescribable peace filled the empty hole that had been there.

New Life, New Adventures (Tiz)

Although I gave my heart to the Lord on the night of February 12, 1976, I never intended to return to that church. I thought, "OK, that was a cool experience," but I figured I'd never see that church again. The next day, however, the pastor and his wife called to invite me back. "I'm sorry," I explained. "I can't go on Sunday because I'm going snow skiing."

"Please come," they said. "Just try it. If you don't like it, go skiing next Sunday. We won't bug you anymore."

Once again, I relented. "I guess I can do that."

"Great! We'll send someone to pick you up. His name is Alex, and he'll be in a VW van."

Sure enough, when Sunday morning rolled around, Alex pulled up outside the dorm, his van crammed with people. When the door swung open, I was introduced to three winos from the streets downtown, a teenage Navajo girl named Esther holding her little newborn baby, and a brother and sister who were of the Hopi people, spoke no English, and were both albino.

All the passengers were quite different from me, but I thought, "I came to Arizona for adventure and to broaden my experiences and relationships. This is definitely all that!"

So I climbed in and squeezed in wherever I could. I was certainly out of my comfort zone. Looking back, it's a miracle that I chose to commit to this new life. But thank God I did. I could not have known all that awaited me on the other side of my yes.

At church that morning the message so moved me that I found myself at the altar again, crying, "God, if this really is You and it's real, I will serve You for the rest of my life. But You've got to show me. I'm going to give it three months, and then I'll know. If it doesn't work out, I'll return to my old life; but if it does, I will serve You forever."

I was born again and serving God! Putting everything else in my life on hold, I dove in, committing to be in church every time the doors were open: morning prayer, Wednesday nights, outreaches—everything. Most nights, we had something going on at church. And God answered my altar prayer. I'd found the missing piece I was seeking. Now I just had to walk it out. Saying yes to God meant saying no to some other things. As I made these choices, God changed my heart, and I fell in love with Him.

God was changing me from the inside out and opening my eyes in new ways. Before I even dated Larry, I became aware of his walk with the Lord. I witnessed his passion for God and compassion for people. I was fascinated with him and watched his every move—the way he prayed and talked about God, the way he talked to people about God, and the way he asked questions to learn from our pastor and the other leaders. I saw Larry's humility and childlike faith. He'd done so many wild and crazy things in his life, yet he was like a little child with the Lord. He was hungry to learn, grow, and become a man of God.

As the three-month caveat to my altar promise expired, I was certain that God was real and that what He was doing was real. Therefore, I planned to serve Him for the rest of my life. I discovered, however, that "he who finds his life will lose it, and he who loses his life for My sake will find it" (Matt. 10:39). That verse describes exactly what happened to me. When I gave my life to the Lord, I felt like I also gave Him my whole identity, along with everything I loved to do and had crafted myself to be. The only thing I could say was "God, You know I'm Yours now. Please make me who You want me to be. I'm not going skiing on Sundays. I'll be in church."

That was a huge commitment and sacrifice for me, because skiing was such a part of my life. Skiing wasn't sinful, and I'd be able to ski again. But if I was going to serve God, I needed to be in church on Sundays. I was in Arizona to find myself, and I did. But I gave up who I had been and gave myself fully to God. A divine exchange occurred. I said, "God, this is who I am. This is what I've accomplished. This is who I think I should be, but I'm trading that for who You want me to be. I'm an open book. Write Your story in my heart."

From that point forward my life took off. However, my parents thought I was in a cult, and my dad wanted to kidnap me and take me back to Montana. At the time, Jim Jones was creating a large following, and Charles Manson's group had been in the news several years before. I couldn't blame my parents for thinking they had to save me. But I wasn't in a cult; I was having a pure experience with the Lord. So I told my parents, "This is what I'm going to do with my life."

They were very scared and worried about me, but it all panned out in time.

Impact of the Sixties and Seventies (Tiz)

Larry and I came from such divergent backgrounds. Yet through the 1960s and 1970s, while he was in inner-city St. Louis and I was in the Rocky Mountains, both of us were influenced in similar ways. The struggles of the times impacted our souls. There were campus protests; friends and loved ones being shipped off to Vietnam; the assassinations of JFK, RFK, and Dr. Martin Luther King Jr.; and the music that reflected all of it.

Although Larry and I grew up very differently, this shared soundtrack reflected our lives. When we came together, that soundtrack bonded us, even though it was mostly from a worldly perspective. The passion of the 1960s and 1970s expressed our desire to make the world a better place. Our zeal reached beyond economic and cultural barriers and impacted who we became as Christians and leaders; it drove us toward feeling unsettled with the status quo and disillusioned with where the world was heading. At times, we tried to initiate change in the wrong ways, but the passion was there. We yearned deeply for something more meaningful than material things. We wanted something beyond what was "normal." Larry wanted to get out of the inner city, and I wanted to find more than I'd found in the Rockies. So we ended up in Flagstaff, Arizona.

The sixties and seventies involved more than being free-spirited, attending concerts, and using drugs. They awakened us to the sense that there was more and that we needed to have a voice and make a difference in the world—the status quo was not an option. This perspective was instrumental in forming Larry and me and in preparing us for what God had in store.

Don't Tell Tiz's Dad (Larry)

TIZ AND I started dating a month after we met, and we got married exactly one year later. If it's God, it's God, and waiting for a prolonged period is not always good. After our relationship got serious, we drove up to Montana to meet Tiz's parents. They were extraordinarily kind and successful people, even knowing that their precious daughter was bringing home a hippie from the hood of South St. Louis who had needle scars on his arms.

Tiz and I had been taught to share our testimony wherever we went. Now Tiz's mom and I were alone in the kitchen, and testimony time had come.

"Tiz tells me you grew up in St. Louis," Tiz's mom said.

"Yeah," I replied, "I grew up in St. Louis." Then I jumped right into my testimony. I started with my street-fighting days in my home city and continued through my drug use, drug dealing, and drug smuggling out of Colombia, South America. I told her how my dad brutally beat us kids and kicked me out of the house. I held nothing back, and I showed Tiz's mom how Jesus changed my life and delivered me from drugs.

With her eyes as wide as saucers, she calmly said, "Whatever you do, don't ever tell Tiz's dad that story." Then she walked out of the kitchen.

To say that Tiz's parents were shocked to see me with their daughter would be a massive understatement. They tried to talk Tiz out of the relationship, but she held her ground, believing I was the one God had for her. And when the dust settled somewhat, we decided to be married at Tiz's aunt's beautiful home in Helena. Little did we know that up till the wedding day, Tiz's dad had told her brother, "If I give you the sign, I'll grab Tiz. You guys grab Larry and hold him back."

That is the truth. We laugh about it now, but the family's fear was real. They had never known or seen a drug addict or a violent man like me. They didn't have a reference point for believing that God could change a life so drastically. Amazingly, the wedding went off without a hitch on February 12, 1977, exactly one year after Tiz gave her life to the Lord.

My Worried Parents (Tiz)

When my parents heard Larry's testimony, they had much fear. In their minds, a junkie would always be a junkie. Illegal drug use was rampant in the 1970s, and every parent had heard the horror stories. My mom and dad didn't know that a person could be supernaturally delivered and transformed. In the natural, someone with a drug habit like Larry's couldn't change. So Mom would say, "What if he goes back to that life? What if he continues to be violent? What if he gets arrested?"

The what-ifs were scary to people who didn't know what the Lord could do. When my mom asked those questions, I replied, "But Larry won't do those things because God has set him free."

My parents were also unhappy that I had uprooted myself and would remain in Flagstaff, with a former junkie, no less. At first they didn't have a chance to get to know Larry. They liked him as a person but were leery of his past. Eventually they fell in love with him. They adored and respected him and saw what great things God had done in our marriage and family. In time Larry and my dad became good friends. And that is a testimony all by itself!

Chapter 10

THE STORY OF OUR LIVES

GOD HAD MIRACULOUSLY delivered me of drugs, but I brought my anger and violence into our marriage. Because of the shame attached to these issues, I never asked anyone for help or insight.

That's what shame does: It keeps us locked in self-defeating patterns for fear of bringing our troubles into the light. We tell ourselves that as Christians, we are not supposed to have those kinds of problems. So when we do, we conclude that something must be terribly wrong with us.

That was my reasoning. So I hid my issues the best I could, until my unexpected outbursts exposed them. I suppressed my rage, but it kept simmering just below the surface. To make things worse, I had no positive role models growing up. I didn't know how to be a godly husband or father. Fortunately, Tiz knew how a family was supposed to function. But it took time for God to teach and transform me.

Shame is a stubborn foe. I've shared publicly what I'm about to say now, but I'm still ashamed to say it. When Tiz was eight months pregnant, I hit her and knocked her down some steps. Shocked at my actions and horrified with what was still inside me, I kept pleading, "I'm sorry! I'm sorry! I'm sorry! Please forgive me."

Thankfully, Tiz was OK. It was an isolated incident, and she forgave me. But she stood up to me, toe to toe, and didn't let me push her around again. I already shared another incident with my son, Luke, when he was four. That's when I knew God had to either free me or kill me, because I couldn't continue the way I was.

This subject is hard to talk about, but it's part of my journey from junkie to Jerusalem. I had other outbursts of anger and rage that kept Tiz walking on eggshells, but she always stayed with me. She's very strong-willed and not a pushover. We had a lot of arguments and fights, but we always chose to say we were sorry, forgive each other, and learn. We also had repentant hearts that wanted to change. We believed in each other, yet beyond that, we believed in God to change us and make us better. And we agreed to do our part in checking our actions and behaviors.

Tiz had every right to leave me back then. But by the sheer grace of God, she stayed until God broke that generational curse and completely set me free. Just as He'd done with the drugs, the Lord snapped the chains of rage and violence that held me. He took my heart, which was hardened by abuse, and He softened it with His supernatural love for others, especially my family. From that day until now, you'd be hard-pressed to make me angry about anything, unless it's anger at the abuse and injustice that others are suffering.

My story is an example of why understanding generational curses is so critical for Christians. I must say this, however: Never tolerate abuse. If you are in an abusive situation that doesn't change, and you can get out, you are justified in leaving. How long you stay in that situation is your decision.

Until God delivered me from anger, I served Him with all my heart, trying my best to contain my anger and repress my violence. God doesn't throw us away because we struggle in certain areas. Yet we must want to get free. I wanted it desperately. I believe with all my heart that God orchestrated Tiz to be in my life—not just anybody, but Tiz. And that's a big part of our story.

Six years ago, when Tiz was diagnosed with ovarian cancer and given three months to live, she defied and overcame the odds. However, several weeks before we started writing this book, she took a turn for the worse and doctors gave her only weeks or days to live. As of this chapter's writing, it's been nearly six months, and she is strong, energetic, and gaining strength day by day. We are seeing the exact opposite of what the doctors said would happen. Tiz is a woman of faith, just as she was early in our marriage. She has the gift of faith. In those early days she understood, as I did, that God didn't make me a drug addict or a violent person. When our grandson Lion got sick, she knew that God didn't give him cancer.

What Satan has meant for evil God will use for good. It goes back to the powerful word *all* in Romans 8:28: "All things work together for good" for those who love God. We could have named this book *Romans 8:28*, because that verse is the story of our lives.

Watching God Work (Tiz)

Let me share the heart of who Larry is. When I first met him, I was physically attracted to him, but what really got me was his spirit and soul. Like he said earlier, our spirits meshed. On top of that, I was absolutely fascinated by him.

Let me explain what I mean. Montana is one of the most gorgeous, wonderful places on the planet. Yet I wanted a life beyond my borders. Hearing about who Larry was and what he had done, plus seeing how God transformed him, was fascinating. I'd never seen or heard anything like his story. It was incredibly compelling, and it made God more real and relatable to me. All I had known were the Christmases and Easters at the Catholic church. I detected no apparent life transformation there. So to hear Larry say, "I was a drug addict, a junkie. I was a drug dealer. And now I'm not," made a huge impact on me. I was also intrigued by Larry as a person and amazed at how the Lord used his testimony to help other people grasp God's power and love for them. Larry's intensity and love for God clearly touched lives. That love was contagious and still is.

In 1976 I'd been a Christian only for a few months. I regularly joined our group at church for an hour of prayer before every service, and each time I arrived, Larry would already be there. I saw his intensity and passion in prayer. Often he'd weep. In other settings he'd give his testimony. At the coffeehouse, bands played and people sat on the floor in a very 1960s and 1970s kind of way. Then Larry would get up and share his story. He'd break up with emotion telling people how Jesus was his first encounter with true love.

People cried as they listened to Larry, and I was deeply moved by what he said. I frequently saw him lending his van to people, giving money to those in need, and praying with people on the streets—completely giving himself to kindness and helping others. I'd never seen anyone do that. But what got to me most was Larry's repentant heart. If he said something hurtful to someone or had an episode of temper, he always repented and turned it around, saying, "God, I'm sorry. Help me not to be this way. I believe You are changing me."

Seeing Larry change in turn changed me. I was on a quest to explore the world, spirituality, and life. Much of that desire came from watching Larry. As we dated and I got to know him better, I understood more of what made him who he was. I saw the miracle of all God had done for him, and it proved that both God and the life He revealed to us were real.

It's important to realize that although I was adventuresome, I was also practical, grounded, and analytical. I wasn't ditzy or lovesick; I had a solid head on my shoulders and always achieved top levels academically. Yes, it occurred to me that my parents could be right about Larry, but I chose to believe that what happened to him was genuine and lasting. I chose to believe that he would never go back to the junkie, drug-dealing lifestyle.

Looking back, my belief was proof of how powerfully the Holy Spirit was working in both of us. God was knitting us together. The world would call it blind faith, but it wasn't blind at all; it was true faith—not in Larry alone but in the God who was at work in him. Even as brand-new Christians, our God experiences were dynamic. The Lord allowed us to rise above the statistics. "Once a drug addict, always a drug addict" was a saying, but God said something different.

Having that foundation beneath us, we then walked through the anger and aggression issues together. Larry wanted to be free, and God wanted to free him. Larry never made excuses or shifted blame for his behavior. He was determined to change; he just didn't know how. But he kept going back to the Lord until the breakthrough came.

Many people in situations like Larry experienced tend to be headstrong. They want to be justified or validated because of circumstances or whatever. In self-defense, they declare, "Well, you made me do it. You made me like this." They never take personal responsibility. That was not Larry's way. He took full responsibility, always repenting to God, asking forgiveness, and making a determined effort to do better. To me, that was huge. The anger and intensity that drove him toward destructive behaviors were redirected in positive, productive ways.

I say all that because I believe it's important for you to see who Larry is. It's been almost fifty years since he surrendered to the Lord, and he still lives every day the way I just described. By the time this book is published, we will have been married forty-eight years and in the ministry almost that long. We have the same heart, soul, and vision for life, family, and ministry; yet we come from completely different backgrounds. Only God could do that.

And so I was born again in that tiny church, and soon after, we were dating. A year after I got born again, Larry and I married. We were both passionate about the Lord and each other, but we had rough edges that needed grinding down and smoothing out. By His grace, God brought out the very best in us.

Those rough times are long gone and behind us. Larry's anger and aggression are either depleted, tamed, or redirected toward the injustices in the world and replaced by compassion for people who are struggling or hurting. Larry is the most genuine, generous, hardworking, fun, bold, fearless, caring man I know. He is the greatest husband, father, and grandfather I could ever imagine. I love and adore him and am so proud of the man he is. If there was an award for the most changed person, I would give it to Larry!

I say this not just to brag on my husband but to boast about our God! Saying yes to Him was the greatest decision we ever made, and it has brought us the adventures of a lifetime.

Another Undeniably Miraculous Prophetic Word (Larry)

When Tiz and I first got married, I was working in construction as a laborer. That's good work until winter comes. In Flagstaff the snow stayed around for months, and all I could get were periodic jobs involving indoor work. Once while I was out of work, an evangelist came to town and spoke at our church. Afterward my pastor, the evangelist, and I had breakfast at Denny's. The evangelist asked me about my work situation. I said, "Man, in wintertime it's hard to get a construction job in Flagstaff."

"What's the best-paying job you've applied for?" he asked.

"Driving trucks for ONC Freight," I told him. ONC delivered supplies all over the West with big semitrucks.

"That's it. God wants you to have it," he said. "Go down and get that job."

"I've applied there several times," I responded. "And I've gone there six or seven times."

"The Lord says that's your job."

"Praise God," I said, as I put a forkful of food in my mouth.

"Why are you sitting here?" he pressed. "Go get it!"

"You mean right now?" I asked.

"Yes! Right now. Go get it right now."

"If you say so," I said.

I left my plate of food on the table and drove to the ONC office. I'd been going there nearly every week for more than a month. When the manager saw me again, she said, "Larry, I told you there are no jobs available. Look at this." She pointed to a stack of applications. "You don't even know how to drive yet. These guys are all experienced drivers—a couple hundred of them. Why would I hire you? I can't do it."

"Listen," I said. "I'll work for free for two weeks loading and unloading trucks. I'll show you I'm the best worker you'll ever have. You can't afford not to hire me."

"I have no openings, Larry."

"I'll work for free," I said. "I'll show you how hard I'll work."

"I'm sorry," she said.

There seemed to be nothing more to say. So I went down the concrete steps with the metal railing, walked to my little Datsun truck, and opened the door to get in. Just then, a man walked out on the platform and yelled, "Did you mean what you said?"

"Excuse me?" I said.

"Did you mean what you said . . . that you'll work hard?"

"I'll work harder than you think," I promised. "I'll be the best worker this company ever had."

"You start Monday," he said.

He was the district supervisor. The offices in that big ware-house had no ceilings, so he had heard my conversation with the manager. He just happened to be there that day—only for an hour to check on things. That's why the evangelist prophet-ically said, "Go now!" Had I gone twenty minutes later, the district supervisor would have been gone.

It pays to discern God's voice and to listen and obey! I started working for the company a couple of days later. Of course, they started me on the night shift. On Wednesday nights we had church. If I was working that night, I would shoot over to church during my dinner hour, all dirty from loading the trucks.

I did that for a while until one day, my supervisor said, "Jump in the semi. We're going to teach you to drive so you can start making runs."

I did what he said. At that point I didn't even know how to

shift gears. I mean, I didn't know anything except that I was a quick learner. I also knew that if God had put me here supernaturally, He would empower me.

Sometimes ONC's eighteen-wheelers had double boxes for hooking up dual trailers. On my first outing, however, I operated a cab with no trailer—what they call *bobtailing*. I drove around the large parking lot and the area surrounding the building. Ten minutes in, I still hadn't gotten out of first gear!

After I had practiced for a few nights, my home phone rang at midnight. It was Sunday, and Tiz and I had just gotten home from church and fellowshipping at Denny's. My boss was calling. "Come down here," he said. "You're making an eight-hour run with a semi—a double rig."

"I haven't even driven with a single rig yet," I said.

"Well, I guess you're going to learn now," he replied.

I got in that semi with a double rig behind me and drove four hours to the destination. We switched boxes, and I drove back another four hours, pulling two trailers. The whole time, both ways, I prayed in the Holy Spirit because I was so scared. The Lord showed up with His peace and assurance to get me through safely. I continued developing my skills, and I drove for another eighteen months or so, making good money. It was God's provision for that season, yet He had a different long-term plan for Tiz and me.

Our first daughter, Anna, was born in May 1978, while I was driving trucks. When she was about a year old, the church leadership offered Tiz and me the opportunity to go into full-time ministry for the church and the denomination. Though it was a huge step of faith, we both got the green light from the Holy Spirit. This was what we had been moving toward since we became Christians. From day one we knew that we would give our lives to see God do for others what He had done for us. Once we told our pastor that we were ready, he said, "Give ONC your two-weeks notice. From now on, you're working for God."

I came on staff as the Flagstaff church's youth director, coffeehouse director, assistant pastor, and chief chair-straightener-upper. Tiz worked side by side along with me in ministry—for no pay. The Lord used her to touch wounded hearts, particularly women's. We were a twofer—two for the price of one! Our pay was a whopping $70 a week (not quite $4,000 for the year), which would amount to about $23,000 annually in today's money. But the amount didn't matter. We were in it for God's kingdom. After a year and a half the leadership said, "We're going to send you to Santa Fe, New Mexico, to start a church."

Though Tiz and I had dissimilar backgrounds, God took our unique giftings and temperaments and brought us together as one to raise a godly family and reach the world for Him. That's what God does. He never wastes anything. He creates us and puts within us what the journey and our destiny in Him require.

A Match Made in Heaven (Tiz)

For two people to be raised completely differently yet share the same kind of strength and forward thinking is miraculous. We needed those qualities to do what we have done. Larry was raised in the streets and by a violent dad. God used those difficulties to drive Larry to become stronger and more than he thought he was. For me, those same characteristics came from a motivational standpoint and were carved out of a hardworking, motivated, loving family rooted in several generations of pioneers. My grandparents and great-grandparents crossed the ocean from Ireland. Then they crossed America in a covered wagon, traveling with their family and children. They lost two children to cholera along the way. I come from tough stock and some tough women.

Larry mentioned that my family was like the Cleavers on *Leave It to Beaver*. That's true in one sense, but the people in my family were also scrappers who fought for everything they had. My parents told me, "Look, the world doesn't owe you anything except an opportunity." From the ground up, I was made to understand that hard work was rewarded. My parents drilled that idea into us kids. So when Larry and I went into the ministry, got involved in business, or did land development on the side, the gutsy, bold entrepreneurship and pioneering of my parents, grandparents, and all the generations that came out West played a part.

I'm not just a sidekick to Larry, and I'm more than a smiling face. I'm as tough as he is but in different ways. I'm a goal-oriented fireball, with a wild, fighting Irish background. I still have that fire within me. But like Larry, I had to tame it. Fire can be wonderfully constructive or utterly destructive. In a lot of ways, Larry and I are different, but when it comes to our drive and dedication, we are the same. We know what we believe, and we are passionate and driven. In the beginning it was just Larry and me, and we were with a church organization. But when they sent us out, it was just us and whichever little babies we had at that point.

God really did put us together as a team. I couldn't be what I am without him, and Larry couldn't be what he is without me. We bring out the best in each other, and we make up each other's differences. Ours is definitely a marriage made in heaven. It needed to be, because as we headed to Santa Fe, we needed each other desperately for the work God had prepared for us.

Chapter 11

SURROGATE PARENTS

THROUGH AN INCREDIBLE chain of miracles, God brought Tiz and me together in Flagstaff, Arizona. I believe He did that because He had a destiny for us as soulmates, or *beshert* to use the Yiddish term. *Beshert* (sometimes spelled *bashert*) literally means "destiny."[1] It's often used to refer to a soulmate or divinely chosen spouse, and if any couple was divinely foreordained, it would be Tiz and me.

Beshert also connotes two halves being joined to make a whole. Although Tiz and I were spiritually whole individuals in Christ and had individual identities, we became one. Our union brought our uniqueness and strengths together to complement one another in life and in the kingdom work to which God called us. *Beshert* took both of us.

Winds of Revival

Victory Chapel, our church in Flagstaff, was planted out of the main church in Prescott, Arizona, and was a part of the Foursquare Church denomination. This area, including Sedona, Arizona, had long attracted spiritual seekers and was a hub for New Age activity. As I mentioned earlier, the Jesus movement swept through Prescott and reached untold numbers of seekers. It became fertile ground for the movement to touch many. When the Jesus movement's refreshing winds blew through Arizona, the members of a popular, upcoming rock band called Eden caught sail and sparked a major youth revival. Eden's lead singer, Ron Burrell, got dramatically born again, went into ministry, and came to Flagstaff to pioneer our church. His move brought the revival to Flagstaff, and God used him tremendously to reach many people, including me.

This movement out of Arizona was similar to what was happening at Calvary Chapel in Costa Mesa, California, with Pastor Chuck Smith. Chuck Smith was very instrumental in birthing the Jesus movement. This movement impacting California and Arizona was sweeping the world. It was breaking out of denominational and religious norms, patterns, boxes, and church buildings. Young people were being saved and dramatically transformed. They were on fire and radical about sharing with others their experiences and relationship with the Lord.

Our churches in Arizona began to raise up and train these young people in leadership and send them out to pioneer new churches. This is what took place with Tiz and me, and we eventually launched out to pioneer our church in Santa Fe, New Mexico. We had a deep passion for the Lord and for people. We wanted our lives to make a difference for God, and what He had done for us, we wanted to help Him do for others. Plus, we received numerous prophetic words going back to when John Metzler prophesied that I would preach around the world.

Church planting was one of the ways God facilitated that prophetic word in our lives. Eventually, we planted seven churches: one in Santa Fe, New Mexico; one in Adelaide, South

Australia; one in Spokane, Washington; one in Melbourne, Australia; two in Portland, Oregon; and one in Dallas, where we are now. Each church had its own mind-blowing God story that will encourage your faith as you read.

Santa Fe Turned Upside Down (Larry)

Santa Fe, New Mexico, is known for its historic adobe architecture, rich Hispanic culture, and stunning landscapes. It's also known for its art galleries, museums, and Native American culture, jewelry, markets, and dance festivals. And don't forget the tourists—lots of tourists.

Santa Fe also has its darker side. Drug addition, alcoholism, street gangs, suicide, and desperation had an entrenched foothold when Tiz and I arrived to plant our first church there in October 1979. We had a vision from the Lord, zeal in our hearts, and a toddler—an only child at the time—clutching our hands. Anna was just eighteen months old; Luke would arrive two years later, in September 1981.

It wasn't always easy, but we decided early on to involve our children in the ministry. We never saw full-time ministry and family as an either-or choice. If God called us to both, we were confident that He would provide, protect, and nurture us and teach us to balance our lives. Growing up, Anna, Luke, and Katie witnessed God's reality and power firsthand. Often they became the vessels the Lord used to touch seemingly untouchable souls.

When Tiz and I kept in step with the Holy Spirit and followed His lead, God was beyond faithful to back us up and even carry us at times. *From Junkie to Jerusalem* is the story of God's absolute realness and faithfulness. We've learned that you can trust God with your life and your kids. You can trust the Holy Spirit to guide you. However, you must follow the direction He gives.

Finding the path of God takes careful discernment so you can know whether or not a word is from Him. Tiz and I never acted on prophetic words alone, but prophecies sometimes added to what we were already sensing. Once we confirmed that a particular word was genuine, we discovered the difference between hearing from the Holy Spirit and acting on what He said. Hearing was not enough; we had to step out in faith and base our shared life on what we heard.

When confirmation came, we acted and brought our kids along for the ride. "The LORD directs the steps of the godly," wrote the psalmist. "He delights in every detail of their lives. Though they stumble, they will never fall, for the LORD holds them by the hand" (Ps. 37:23–24, NLT). Psalm 37 encapsulates our ministry and family story to this day. We simply believe it and walk in it. We trust God's direction and how He upholds us, even when we make mistakes.

Our young family had its own dynamics, as every family does. Tiz was our navigator. I really leaned on her and trusted her. Her parents and grandparents showed her what a healthy family looked like, and the Holy Spirit was (and is) her guide. I'm not saying we never had family issues to work through. We did. But our hearts were set on pleasing the Lord and raising our children in His ways. Yes, we took our kids into some hard places to do ministry, but Tiz and I tried to never let the ministry come before them. Although we made some mistakes along the way, all our kids serve the Lord and even work with us in the ministry.

Now, that's a testimony! I share it here because it's important to know that even with children, we ministered where we were called: in the most challenging areas. We've never served in nice, conservative, suburban neighborhoods or pastored in already established churches. We've gone straight to the toughest streets to reach the down-and-out. They're our priority, and we established churches so their lives could be turned around. Each time, we knew that if we were faithful to reach them, the Lord would send other people from the city to stand with us.

The first thing we did in Santa Fe—even before we found our little flat—was to find a building to hold services. In the barrio (the roughest part of the Hispanic neighborhood), we found a run-down, vacant building that once housed Henry's Liquor and Meat Market. The place had iron bars on the windows, holes in the floor and roof, and graffiti on the walls and windows. My office was in a big beer and meat cooler with a heavy door, and the smell in there wasn't the best.

The building had plenty of history. While Henry's was still operating, gangbangers regularly broke in and robbed the place. One night after the owner decided that enough was enough, he waited in the shadows with a shotgun. When the thieves broke in, he shot and killed one of them. He went to prison for the killing, and the business shut down. No one dared to open another business there, so the building just deteriorated. When we saw it, we were ecstatic. "This is perfect!" we said. "It's just what we need."

Right across the street, a river ran through the barrio, and five or six young crack addicts lived under the bridge. I went over, shared my testimony with them, and invited them to church. The crack addicts gave their lives to the Lord and were our first members—and our first volunteers! I told them, "As long as you guys are here, why don't you be my ushers?"

This story might sound foolish to the world and the religious crowd, but most of those addicts continued serving God, and several ended up in the ministry. The amazing, life-transforming power of the gospel is simple but real. Before Tiz and I arrived, local drug dealers used that building as their meeting place. All night, every night, kids did drug deals in the parking lot. They smoked, shot up drugs, and engaged in other shadowy activities.

Tiz and I focused on those kids and began working with them. They tried to continue their usual activities, but with the building occupied, we were able to shut down the chaos. We didn't have to go looking for kids to reach. They were already there, waiting to hear the good news that would heal their searching hearts. Many of them had no family. The rest were in highly dysfunctional families. Most of their dads, brothers, cousins, and even moms were in prison, so we became like surrogate parents. One by one, the kids gave their lives to the Lord, and revival began.

A few nights before our grand opening, a group of gang-bangers asked, "Hey, what are you doing?"

They wanted the signs. I said, "All right, I'll make you a deal. I'll give you these beer signs if you come to church."

"OK," they said, and we made the trade. One of the boys, named Raymond, said, "All right, Father Huch, what time is mass?"

As it turned out, Raymond became one of our main young men. He was only a teenager. His father and older brothers were in prison. He and his mom, his younger brothers, and his sisters lived in the house next door to the church. Raymond was with us pretty much all the time.

With only young male and female gangbangers in our congregation, the church exploded in growth. Often, the girls were more brutal than the boys. One gal, Patsy, headed up a serious boys' gang that carried guns and knives—the whole deal. Patsy had suffered multiple gunshot wounds through her abdomen and was stabbed several times. Most of her teeth were missing because she once jumped off a bridge in a suicide attempt. Patsy's body was scarred, and she was as tough as nails. Yet the Holy Spirit broke through her toughness, and she gave her life to the Lord. To help her get established, we took her closely under our wing, and the Lord transformed her life. She even got married and became a powerful leader in our church.

We took in several wayward young guys to live in our seven-hundred-foot flat. It got pretty crowded at times, but that didn't matter. Tiz was the mom they never had. She made them meals, looked out for them, and taught them about the Lord and life. Mostly, she loved on them. When the flat got too tight, we rented the flat next to ours and turned it into the boys' home. Fifteen or twenty guys piled in there, all of them ex-druggies. Eventually, we needed a third flat for a girls' home, and it was also packed.

Tiz and I took in these kids and mentored them. We helped them find jobs and cultivate productive lifestyles. They called us Mom and Dad. We loved them but held them accountable. They knew they had to toe the line, and if they went into the bars, we'd find them. There were moments when love had to be tough, but the kids respected us for it and reaped the rewards of change. It's amazing how a human mind is transformed when the Holy Spirit comes in and addictions are broken. He recalibrates a person's entire mindset. All these young people were on fire for God and went back to the streets with us to reach others and tell them about the power of God to change their lives.

The religious community and those who were making money off the system hated us. But God was using a passionate, delivered ex-junkie and a passionate, Spirit-filled Rocky Mountain woman to run drugs out of the barrio. Word spread like wildfire, and in three years we saw six thousand teenagers come to Jesus.

Judges called us, saying, "Listen, I got these kids. I hate to put them in jail. Do you want to take them?"

We said, "Yes." So these judges actually sentenced these kids to do time at our church, Victory Chapel, under our supervision!

Youth from the streets hung around us everywhere. Tiz and I poured our hearts and lives into our people, and the love was contagious. It was like *The Cross and the Switchblade*[2]—David Wilkerson kind of stuff—an authentic move of God that was way bigger than us.

Victory Chapel took over that old, run-down liquor store, and our kids chipped in to completely remodel it. They took ownership and made it their church. While there was seating for about 150 people, we could jam in up to 200, packing it out every Sunday and for other services throughout the week. We also held outdoor services in the park across the street, which always drew good crowds.

When we outgrew our building, we moved into an abandoned bar/strip club, cleaned it out (physically and spiritually), and made it our church. Young people from diverse backgrounds worked to remodel it, and it became a beautiful and cool place to worship God. This building sat five hundred people, and we packed that out as well. By that time many families joined us, so we had young people, ex-gang members and drug dealers, moms and pops, entire families, grandparents, Hispanics, Pueblo Native Americans, and even some white people (including our own growing family).

We preached God's Word, which filled the people's hearts and minds and laid a foundation for their lives. Isaiah wrote, "So shall My word be that goes forth from My mouth; it shall not return to Me void, but it shall accomplish what I please, and it shall prosper in the thing for which I sent it" (Isa. 55:11). We saw that verse fulfilled in our midst. The worship was simple, with no bells and whistles, but the enthusiasm and love were infectious. I led by singing, and Tiz played a small electric piano. When she knew we would pioneer a church, she learned three chords and told herself, "Somebody's got to play the piano or organ. So I guess I'd better learn."

That's the kind of person Tiz is. She used a magic marker to write the three chords on the keys, and it worked! The diverse voices in our multicultural congregation blended as one and glorified God. Over time, God added musicians and singers to our worship team. It was a beautiful thing. What we lacked in polish, we made up for in passion. The Holy Spirit was in the house! Every service was electric with excitement, joy, and lives being changed. That's a powerful combination, whatever your ethnicity.

Jesus said, "You shall know the truth, and the truth shall make you free" (John 8:32). That's exactly what happened: A continual stream of people came and gave their lives to the Lord. He set them free, and they found acceptance, love, and a new path in life. Romans 2:11 tells us that God shows no partiality. Most of our congregation came from the barrio, but if they'd come from Wall Street, the effects of truth on their souls would have been the same. Our services were full of life and zeal and were a bit on the wild side. We had fun at our church picnics, campouts, and baptisms at the Pecos River in the gorgeous mountains outside Santa Fe. We were an electric and eclectic church family!

While we were in Santa Fe, the Lord opened the door for me to do miracle healing services in Mexico and the Philippines. God moved in incredible ways, and I got a taste of the international and global call. We also held local healing services on the Navajo reservation. We saw many miracles at those services and made great friends in the Navajo community.

The United Nations for Christ

From the beginning a huge part of our story has involved breaking down the racial and cultural barriers that divide people. Our church in Santa Fe brought together many groups that didn't typically gather with one another. It was in Santa Fe that we dug in our heels and said, "We will be the United Nations for Christ."

Those words sound great when people say them, but not everyone likes putting the idea into practice. Probably six months after starting Victory Church, we met a white couple and felt a real connection with them. When they learned we were pastors, they said, "Oh, man, we've been looking for a church." The next Sunday, they came to the service.

Afterward they remarked, "We didn't know the congregation was almost all Hispanic and Native people."

"Yeah," we said. "That's who we are."

"Well, that's not done here."

I countered, "I guess that's why God sent us."

They never came back.

We have faced similar mindsets and barriers in every city we've been in, including in Australia. Pioneering churches is hard in other ways, especially when you are dealing with kids who are violent, angry, on drugs, and lacking adult figures in their lives. As hard as it is, it's also fun, adventuresome, and rewarding. Most importantly, the churches we pioneered made a lasting impact.

Tiz and I went back to Santa Fe a couple of years ago, more than forty-five years after we'd been in that old church. When we introduced ourselves to the owner of the art framing shop that now occupies the building, he said, "I know exactly who you are. People still talk about those days because of the influence you had in this neighborhood. A lot of the kids who were in your church are now leaders in the community and have helped to change things by running youth programs and other community efforts."

Tiz and I already knew about some of the people who had entered the ministry. We poured our hearts and souls into that church family and never thought we would leave Santa Fe, where our own family grew. However, the group of churches was branching out into Australia, and Tiz and I felt the Lord calling us to start a church there. Leaving Santa Fe was incredibly difficult because we loved the congregation so much. But after saying our tearful goodbyes, we turned Victory Chapel over to another pastor and launched out to Adelaide, South Australia.

Uprooting all that is familiar and moving to another country is not easy. But the Lord was with us every step of the way. And once again, revival broke out.

Miracles in Adelaide, South Australia

In January 1983 we packed up our belongings and our two kids and moved to Australia to pioneer a church. The culture and customs of Adelaide were unlike anything we'd known, but our strategies were the same: love and acceptance. We found an old bank building down the street from our house. It was small and in rough shape, but it was easy to reach from home.

Once again Tiz and I had to clean and paint the place before we could hold services. A few days before our opening, we and the kids walked to the church carrying flyers about our inaugural service. As we approached an aboriginal family on the way, they backed up against the wall and looked down at the ground. At first we thought they didn't understand English, so we pointed down to the building and back to the flyer, hoping to communicate somehow. Still refusing to look into our eyes, they inched away and pretended not to understand.

Two days later we opened the church with the movie *The Cross and the Switchblade*.[3] Halfway through the film, the aboriginal family walked in, and the next night they returned with more people. As they entered, they immediately stood against the back wall. I tried to offer them chairs, but they looked down and shook their heads, saying, "No, no, no."

We learned that communication between aboriginal and white people was basically considered taboo. I didn't care and gave a big bear hug to the grandmother in the family (the matriarch in that culture). Then I sat her down in a chair, sat on her lap, wrapped my arms around her neck, and kissed her cheek! The whole family burst into laughter until tears ran down their happy faces.

Well, that was it—we were family, and they were in for life. The barrier came down, and hundreds of aboriginal people eventually came to the church.

As we'd done before, we chose to reach people in the worst neighborhoods. Australia's streets were like American streets: Drugs, violence, and racism were rampant. In the hearts of cities like Adelaide and Melbourne, neighborhoods were divided into Chinese, Russian, Ukrainian, and other sections, depending on which nationalities were present, and nobody interacted. Street and business signs were written in the various languages.

In Adelaide heavy racism kept people from mixing. We

thought, "OK, this is where we need to be," and we broke down those walls. The grace of God brought people in, but it was our acceptance and love that kept them there.

Just as in Santa Fe, the services were simple, but the atmosphere of love was contagious. And by this time, Tiz knew four chords on the electric piano! The church grew and continued growing. Regardless of ethnicity, everyone mingled together for morning prayer meetings, parties, barbecues, and all kinds of events and gatherings. The aboriginal people we reached spread the word among their tribes that there were white people who loved them.

A little aboriginal lady in our church was missing most of her fingers and many of her toes, and her face and body were scarred—the result of leprosy she had suffered as a child. She'd been raised in a leper colony, but God healed her of the disease. We called her Aunty Betty, and she became our kids' surrogate grandma. Imagine seeing a black-skinned aboriginal woman cuddling our fair-skinned kids in a racially divided Australia. It was unheard of!

Years later an Australian TV commercial showed a little white girl on a swing as an aboriginal child walked by, followed by an Asian child and an island child. When the white child's mother came for her and they walked away together, the child asked, "Mummy, what color is Jesus?" Her mom replied, "Honey, Jesus is the light of the world, and pure light is made up of every color in the rainbow."

I'm convinced that our church's impact in breaking down racial barriers at least partially inspired this commercial. To this day I can feel Aunty Betty hugging me and remember her finger nubs pressing my neck and face as she kissed my cheek. God bless her—she was a soul winner who loved God. As of this writing, Aunty Betty is in her nineties, and after forty years, we remain in touch with her.

Australia is a large country, and most of its big cities are on the continent's perimeter. The whole middle territory is the outback, and in its center are the aboriginal reserves. A government-funded program regularly bused aboriginal people into the city, where they bought groceries and other goods and stayed in hostels before returning home. At the people's request, the buses also drove them to our church, because the people heard about a white couple who loved and accepted them. God touched their lives deeply, and that love spread and multiplied. The idea was revolutionary at that time. Almost the same thing happened in all the other cities where Tiz and I pastored. People visited the church and said, "Wow, this is never done in Australia."

And always, we responded, "Well, it is now. That's why God sent us here."

Fortunately, aboriginals are more respected and accepted in Australia now. The change didn't happen overnight, and neither did our story. There was no quick effort or flukish event that "just happened." The path has all been very deliberate and Spirit-led.

Tiz's Mom and a Divine Dream

One night a few months after we settled in Adelaide, a nightmare woke me up, shaking and in a cold sweat. When I fell back asleep, the nightmare returned. My tossing and turning awakened Tiz.

"What's wrong, Larry?" she asked.

"I keep having this nightmare of somebody drowning," I said. "I see them being sucked down in a whirlpool."

The dream happened three or four times that night. The

last time it came, I stayed up until just before dawn and then went back to bed.

"Are you OK?" Tiz asked, trying to comfort me.

"I had that nightmare again," I replied. "Someone going down in the whirlpool cried out, 'Jesus, help me!' And suddenly a hand reached into the whirlpool and snatched the person out."

"What do you think that means?" wondered Tiz.

"I have no idea," I said. "But it kept me up praying and praying."

Adelaide is on the ocean, so I thought the dream might be a warning to stay away from the water. Eventually I told Tiz, "I don't know what the dream means, but whatever it is, it's OK. I felt it lift."

Our church had a 6 a.m. prayer meeting, and I asked one of the guys to open the building so I could go back to bed. About thirty minutes later a couple of church people knocked on our door. "Pastor," they said, "we were down at the church, and the phone rang. It was the United States consulate. You need to call home right away at this number. There's been an emergency."

It was Tiz's dad's number. "Something's happened to my dad," Tiz said. But when we called, he was the one who answered.

He explained that Tiz's mom, Gwen, was driving to another city to meet with the senator for whom she worked when a semitruck crossed into her lane and hit her head-on. The driver was past his legal limit for consecutive driving hours and had drugged himself to keep going. Then he fell asleep and drifted into Gwen's lane.

Tiz's aunt worked for Gwen and was following her in a separate car. Within minutes of the accident, she came upon the crash site. Tiz's brother, who worked for the highway department, also came to the scene. When he realized his mom was involved, he called his dad to the site.

We learned later that Gwen was alive and pinned inside the car, which was trapped under the semi for several hours. Her body was nearly severed, and the pressure of the vehicle against her body kept her alive. As soon as the Jaws of Life pulled the car away, however, her life on earth ended.

I remembered that as we prepared to move to Australia, we had decided to take the kids and visit Tiz's folks before we left the States. On one of our nights in Montana, we sat with Tiz's parents until around midnight, talking to them about the Lord and why we do what we do. They were Catholic and trying to understand the biblical concept of being born again, asking Jesus into your heart, and having a personal, intimate relationship with the Lord. Tiz's dad eventually said, "Well, I'm going to bed."

When he left, Tiz's mom said, "Well, I'm not ready to pray and ask Him into my heart right now. But you're saying that at any point or time I could pray and ask Jesus into my heart, and I don't have to go through a confessional or a priest?""

We said, "No, Mom, just call out to Him wherever you are."

Several months later, at Gwen's funeral, a nurse told Tiz that one of the EMTs at the scene of Gwen's accident was this nurse's good friend. "My friend crawled into the wreck and stayed with your mom," she said. "For several hours your mom was in and out of consciousness."

The nurse continued, "My friend, the main EMT, stayed with your mom as much as possible while the Jaws of Life tried to free her from the smashed car as your dad, brother, and aunt watched in shock and horror. She and the EMT team knew that Gwen was literally hanging on by a thread of life. Suddenly, Gwen moaned heavily and whispered to the

EMT, 'I'll be OK. Tell Tiz I'll be all right. She'll know.' Those were the last words she spoke. Shortly later, when the Jaws of Life finally dislodged the car off her body, she passed into the loving arms of the Lord."

We figured out that this happened at the same time I had my dream. Years later when we told the story to his dad, he was very touched and eventually gave his life to the Lord.

My Grace Is Enough (Tiz)

When my mom died, I was devastated. I was only twenty-seven, and we'd been in Australia only for six months. This move turned our whole life upside down. Everything was new, and I was still getting my bearings when I lost my mom. We returned for her funeral but were in Helena only for a week. Then we returned to Adelaide and were immediately back in church.

I did my best to carry on. I strove to be there for the church in Adelaide while being a mother to my kids and a wife to Larry. But one day after church I went home, collapsed in a corner of our bedroom, and sobbed and sobbed. I was so grief-stricken and broken that I didn't know whether I could go on. That's when the Lord gently spoke to my heart from 2 Corinthians 12:9: "My grace is sufficient for you, for My strength is made perfect in weakness." Of course, the key to this verse is in the previous verses. The Lord told Paul about His grace *after* Paul pleaded with Him to remove whatever his thorn in the flesh was.

Because of what Larry and I had been taught, I had the impression that the Lord was reprimanding Paul and saying, "It's enough. My grace is enough for you. Don't be asking Me for more. Shape up."

With that picture in mind, I looked at God in a certain way. So, amid my grief, I said, "OK, Lord, I'll pull it together. I'll be OK."

Then, with an almost audible voice, the Lord whispered in my soul, "No, no. I'm saying that My grace is enough for you. My grace will help, equip, and carry you through. I've got you."

At that moment the words of Corrie ten Boom's sister, Betsie, came to mind. Nearing death in the Ravensbrück concentration camp, she reminded Corrie, "There is no pit so deep that He [God] is not deeper still."[4] I recognized God's love and understood that He wasn't reprimanding me or telling me to shape up. He was consoling, loving, and equipping me to rise above my grief.

Weeping uncontrollably, with my body tucked like a ball in the corner of that room, I felt the Holy Spirit fill me, as though warmth flowed down and inside my soul and deep in my heart. My tears of grief became tears of joy, and God's presence overtook my grief. Suddenly I realized what was possible, and I prayed, "God, I believe that whatever I have lost with my mom's death—all that joy, love, and the wonderful family life that we had—You will multiply it back to my family."

Assurance and peace filled me. I can't say that the grief was over, but I went to a new place in God that day. I knew that He would handle my family's future, everything would be good, and He would multiply back to my family everything we had lost. That revelation and experience of God's grace, love, and help changed and shaped my view of Him forevermore.

One Person at a Time (Larry)

Concerning the pioneering of churches, especially in other countries—I mean, really, how do you do that? You don't know anyone. You don't know the culture. You don't even know where to start in a city of a million and a half people. So how in the world do you reach people?

The Lord put this answer in our hearts: "You do it the same way you've done everything else—one by one. You don't try to reach a nation. You go and reach one person at a time."

When we first arrived in Adelaide, Tiz and the kids went to a store to buy some furniture. The salesman asked Tiz, "What's that accent?"

"We're from America," she answered.

"Well, what are you doing here?" he asked.

She told him that we were starting a church, and he said, "Wow, my wife and I just talked this week about how we need to get God back in our lives. Can we come to your church?"

"Are you kidding?" Tiz said. "Of course you can come!"

The furniture salesman and his wife came to our services and became one of our foundational couples. In fact, we received a letter from the husband a couple of weeks ago, asking, "Remember me?"

We've learned that God goes before us. And when we step out in faith to obey, He maps out our steps and provides all the people and resources we need. Then, as we trust Him, His plan unfolds.

Another key story from Adelaide is about Mick and Michelle, rugged bikers with tatted-up faces and bodies. Michelle had endured a lot. When she was eleven years old, she saw her father shoot her mother dead. He went to prison, and Michelle ended up in foster homes that turned out badly. After running away repeatedly, she lived on the streets as a teenager. To support herself, she turned to drug dealing and prostitution.

On one occasion Michelle overdosed and lay comatose in an abandoned building for three days. Because one of her legs was on top of the other, the bottom leg atrophied and became gangrenous. Eventually someone found her and took her to a hospital, where her atrophied leg was amputated and she remained in a semicomatose state for several months. When she regained consciousness, her remaining leg was paralyzed. From that point on, Michelle lived in a wheelchair, yet she returned to the streets and to prostitution.

Both she and Mick were as tough as bikers could be. Somehow Mick would secure Michelle's wheelchair to the back of the bike, and then Michelle would slide behind him on the motorcycle's seat and hold on. That's how they rolled.

Mick and Michelle came into our church the night we showed the movie *The Cross and the Switchblade*. They both ended up at the altar and gave their lives to the Lord. When we started to pray with them, though, Michelle pushed us away and said, "Don't touch me!" So I focused on Mick, and Tiz approached Michelle, explaining that we cared and wanted to help them.

"Nobody cares about me!" Michelle snapped. "You don't care about me. Nobody does. Don't touch me. Just leave me alone."

We still prayed for them, but they remained stoic, shedding no tears and showing no emotion. Then they left, and we thought they would never come back.

However, the next night, they showed up again, affirmed their relationship with the Lord, bonded with us, and cried their eyes out. We spent a long time with them, and they became a leading couple in our church. They called us their mom and dad and were involved in everything we did the whole time we were in Adelaide. They were at our house all the time and were very powerful in winning souls to the Lord.

In just three years' time, our church in Adelaide ministered to forty-two nationalities and interpreted messages into twelve or thirteen languages. Our church family included Russians, Yugoslavians, Italians, Ukrainians, Chinese, Indians, aboriginals, Hungarians, Germans, Aussies, and even a few American folks from the Huch family, all worshipping and growing in the Lord.

A Supernatural Encounter
Right Before Their Eyes

Nevertheless, we began feeling the tug to return to the States, particularly to the Pacific Northwest and the mountains. So when the leaders of our sending church presented the opportunity to start a church in Spokane, Washington, we took them up on the offer. Despite having to say tearful goodbyes and uproot again, we knew the Holy Spirit was guiding us. Looking back, it was all part of getting us where He ultimately wanted us to be.

As we had done in Santa Fe and Adelaide, we went into the tough neighborhoods where nobody else would go. We poured our hearts into those areas of Spokane with the same kinds of results we'd had elsewhere: Lives were set free and transformed by God's love.

Amazingly, as the church became established, our leadership shared with us their desire to build another church in Australia. Because we had been so effective in Adelaide, they wanted us to do it again in Melbourne. Just before they asked this of us, I read an article about the city claiming that ten thousand kids were hitting Melbourne's streets every day and that most of them were heroin addicts. The article grieved my heart. Since the invitation back to Australia seemed like more than a coincidence, I told Tiz, "Let's go back. Let's go reach these kids."

So we told the leadership, "OK, we'll go back."

And we did. We knew we would be homesick for America and our roots. But we always felt that our lives were not our own, and we saw the sacrifice of our lives as our reasonable service (Rom. 12:1). God always made the difficult choices more than worthwhile, so off we went to start a church in Melbourne, Victoria. And just as we'd done several times before, we found a vacant property so we could start reaching the kids on the streets.

Our Melbourne encounters got really Spirit-filled, and fast! We were in the suburb of Dandenong, a quaint community with some rough sections. For example, there was a vacant train station where kids came by the hundreds to do drugs, leaving the ground covered with needles and filth. We'd go there, climb up on a bench or table with a portable PA system, and assure them, "It doesn't matter who you are or where you're from. Jesus loves you."

Afterward some of the kids who had already given their hearts to the Lord would share their testimonies. One such night, one of our young guys, an Aussie, shared what Jesus had done for him. Since he had a history as a party-and-drug guy, all the addicts listened to him. But just as he said, "Jesus loves you," I saw out of the corner of my eye someone throw a whiskey bottle at him. Before I could warn him, the bottle that was headed right for the speaker stopped in midair and shattered.

We had witnessed something supernatural, and hundreds of people saw it. When we gave an altar call, about a hundred kids gave their lives to Jesus. This is not an inflated number. Then these young converts followed us to the church, where we baptized them in a horse trough filled with water. It was wild!

We decided that the Melbourne church would become another United Nations for Christ, and because of that, we reached many nationalities. We had people from Hungary, Germany, Samoa, Belgium, South America, Russia, Ukraine, and other parts of Europe, along with Tonga, Mauritius, and Indonesia.

Until They Know You Care

One of our church members brought in Fred, an older man from the streets who had been homeless most of his adult life. Fred gave his life to the Lord, and some of the families took him in. When we heard that his birthday was coming, we threw a party for him at the church. A Hungarian lady made a cake, and we all gathered around Fred, wishing him well.

Fred just cried and cried. "This is the first birthday cake I've ever had, and I'm seventy-five years old today," he said.

Lives are changed when people know you care. When many ask us, "Why do you care about us?" we usually answer, "Because we've been there. We've lived life. We've been boots on the ground in ministry for almost fifty years and have experienced some things. We really and truly care."

The famous saying is that people don't care how much you know until they know how much you care. This truth describes our experiences in ministry. Even as our influence has grown, individuals are still the issue. Jesus was all about leaving the ninety-nine to rescue the one, like Patsy or Aunty Betty. He was there when Tiz's mom called out to Him from under a semitruck. He even gave me that terrible dream so I could pray for her.

The Lord sees you. He hears your cries and your painful thoughts. He knows what you're going through, and He wants to show up with His comforting and empowering presence. All you have to do is let Him in.

Chapter 12

BACK TO AMERICA
AND THEN...

W HEN WE FIRST agreed to go to Melbourne, we agreed that we would give about three years to the work there and then ask the Lord to open a door for us in the States. Our third child, Katie, was born in Melbourne. As an added blessing, she was born on Tiz's mom's birthday, which was a gift from God. We knew we wouldn't spend the rest of our lives in Australia. So we poured our hearts into serving Melbourne, knowing we would soon return to America.

Having grown up in Montana, Tiz had the mountains in her blood. They got into my bloodstream too, but we needed to be where people were. So when an opportunity arose to build a church in Portland, Oregon, we jumped at it. Portland is situated along the picturesque Columbia River, in the shadow of the Cascade Range.

It was 1988 when we settled in Portland. Anna was nine, Luke was five, and Katie was eighteen months. Portland was new to us, but we repeated our pattern: We went into the streets, found the down-and-out, broke down barriers, crossed racial and economic divides, and bridged the gap. It didn't matter whether people were homeless, shirtless, shoeless, alcoholic, drug-addicted, black, white, yellow, red, rich, or poor. All were welcome, and that's who came.

Our church in the Portland area was a bit of a hybrid: It had a feel and spirit similar to David Wilkerson's Times Square Church and Tommy Barnett's Dream Centers in Phoenix and Los Angeles. In addition to the down-and-out, we had many "regular" families and some up-and-comers. Many of the players on our women's softball team, which won the city championship three years in a row, were ex-lesbians. They came into the church and never felt condemnation. They felt compelled to let God transform their lifestyles.

We taught God's Word without compromise, but the people knew we weren't judging them. They knew that when the Lord rescued me, I had seven warrants out for my arrest and needle marks up and down my arms. They knew He didn't tell me to go get cleaned up and then come. They believed it when we said that Christianity is a come-as-you-are gathering. We told them what Jesus says: "Come to Me, all you who labor and are heavy laden, and I will give you rest. Take My yoke upon you and learn from Me, for I am gentle and lowly in heart, and you will find rest for your souls" (Matt. 11:28–29).

We invited people to come as they were, knowing God would do the cleaning up. We simply served Him and His people as one big family. As you can imagine, many folks didn't like that approach. Some took exception to our redemptive and multiracial church. Leaders in the area told me, "If you try to build a church like that here, it will cost you."

"Well then, it'll cost us," I said.

Building a multiracial, nonjudgmental congregation doesn't happen automatically. It takes being intentional. We started in a small storefront building in Oregon City, grew into a larger building, and soon had to hold three services on Sundays. All kinds of people came, and many young people gave their lives to the Lord. The atmosphere was electric and filled with contagious love.

After several months in Portland, Tiz and I chose to leave our group affiliation and become nondenominational. We were thankful for all we had learned and all the opportunities the sending church had given us, but we felt the Lord was leading us into another level of ministry and influence. So we broke away and renamed and restarted our church as New Beginnings. We searched out other godly leaders and pastors and set ourselves on a quest to expand our thinking, knowledge, and ways of ministering and pastoring.

When we made the move—*boom!* New Beginnings Church grew so fast that we had to hire a full staff and more. We also developed an anointed worship team to hand that part of the services off to. Growth brought changes, but we remained true to what had gotten us to this point. We stuck with the solid teaching of God's Word, the anointing of the Holy Spirit on everything we did, and our commitment to love people.

In several years, the church grew to more than five thousand and impacted the city in profound ways. We quickly outgrew our building, moved to another, and then outgrew it too. We adopted a saying, "Here we grow again!" The atmosphere of our services was electric, and the impact in our communities was extensive and ongoing.

We made it a point to take the church outside the four walls. Tiz put up signs in the lobby above the exit doors that said, "You are now entering the harvest field!" We had many life groups pouring their energy into the communities. We cleaned up school campuses and did outreaches. On Saturdays our men set up their tools and equipment at the church, and single moms or anyone in need brought their cars for tune-ups, oil changes, or detailing. We went to people's homes (particularly the elderly) to clean, mow the grass, and help them with repairs.

As always, our goal was to break down the walls of division based on race, socioeconomic status, age, or culture. We were the United Nations of Christ—one big, eclectic family! We created dynamic ministries for all age groups and for those fighting addiction or dysfunctional lifestyles. Our church motto became, "No matter who you are, where you've come from, or what you've done, Jesus has a new beginning for you."

We became known as a church for "those kind of people," meaning those who were down and out. This was true, but our church was also full of "up-and-outers" too. People from all walks of life sat together, prayed together, and loved one another. We truly were coming together as one big family. It was incredible!

We built a team that worked like clockwork. The church was a lean, mean machine, and we were changing lives, our city, and the world at the same time!

Tiz and I continued to include our kids in ministry. We never dragged them to church to sit in the pews as spectators. We always involved them in a genuine relationship with God and with the people in the church. As a result they have helped us form and build various ministries over the years— for children, youth, young adults, and the churches. I'm so proud of our kids and their spouses!

Even our grandkids are involved in the ministry and changing people's lives, and we could not be prouder. They all totally and wholeheartedly serve God, love people, and are very involved in all that God is doing. Our kids have a heart and compassion for people because our family has been where they are. We know what God can do for them because He did it for us. He broke generational curses and tore down the walls in my heart. He healed my painful memories with my earthly father and replaced them with the intimate experiences of knowing my heavenly Father. He taught me to be a loving and caring person able to cultivate deep relationships and raise godly children.

God forever changed my future and our family's future. The fruit of His grace toward us is evident every day. But we are proudest of how we have served as a family. Our family is our greatest joy. They are our best friends and our greatest partners in ministry.

Ministry to Pastors

One day at a conference in Texas, the Holy Spirit spoke to my spirit and said, "I want you to reach out to struggling pastors." During a break, I was in the men's restroom and a pastor introduced himself to me. I immediately told him that I was going to have a conference for pastors and asked him if he would like to come, at our expense. He said, "Well, of course! When is the conference?" I said, "I don't know yet. God just told me to do it."

I held that word in my heart and let it take root. But I immediately told Tiz and the staff, "We're going to start a conference and invite pastors who are struggling or have fallen. We will cover their airfare and hotel costs, and we'll feed them. We're going to reach out and restore them. We as a staff and church family are going to be an extension of God's hands, feet, and heart."

We invited twenty pastors and their wives to our first

conference. In time, we invited and hosted hundreds of pastors at a cost of half a million dollars per conference—money we didn't have. Still, we felt the calling to invest in pastors. The last conference we held in Portland included about three hundred couples. We always put up a big tent to serve meals and encourage the pastors. Tiz and I went from table to table, kneeling around our guests while talking and ministering to them.

Pastoring is a tough gig. We've all been to conferences where the big shots were pampered in the big-shot room and the nobodies made do outside with peanuts and tap water. We wanted to show wounded and weary pastors how special they were. The big names came to speak, but six or seven hundred volunteers took time off from work to serve our invitees as the hands, feet, and heart of Jesus. They met the couples at the airport, cheered them as they deplaned, and served them all week long.

The denominations and backgrounds of our guests didn't matter to us. We started the conference to be redemptive toward them. I already mentioned how the shepherd leaves ninety-nine sheep to find the missing one. But as I told our congregation, "Who goes after the shepherds when they get lost? Let's reach out to pastoral couples who are having difficulty."

At one pastors' conference, I preached about not giving up but pressing in to all that God has for you. By inspiration of the Holy Spirit, I said "If you're a pastor in the process of a divorce and God is speaking to you about calling to cancel that divorce tomorrow, I want you and your wife to stand up. We're going to pray for you."

Sixty-eight couples responded, recommitted to each other, and canceled their divorces! Yet some denominational leaders told their people, "If you go to that conference, we'll rescind your license." They said, "God is trying to clean out the body of Christ, and Huch's holding onto all the garbage."

Hearing that, I thought, "God never looks at us that way." When I was a drug addict, He didn't see me as garbage. He saw my future. We often run into people who say, "I was at that conference. You helped us, and we're still in the ministry. We're still married because you reached out to us."

Hearing those comments pours fuel on the fire in our souls. People often contacted us and said, "I've got this friend in South Carolina," or "We've got these people in New York, and they're getting ready for a divorce. The wife's back on drugs," or whatever the story was. Ministry can be lonely and make you feel like a loser. When we heard about people's struggling friends, we invited them to come and paid their way. Many of them didn't know how to respond. They didn't know us or New Beginnings. It sometimes took a couple of days for them to grasp why two strangers were offering to help.

I can't tell you how many couples suspected us of being a cult or pyramid scheme. Yet they were hurting so badly that they came anyway and found two fellow pastors who knew what their struggle was like. Tiz always says that being a friend is often the most spiritual thing we can do. Pastoring is an emotionally demanding gig. The pastors we served were lonely, wounded, weary, or struggling in some way. They came from every background, denomination, and race, and we helped them focus, believe in themselves, and enlarge their faith in God.

So many pastors who were discouraged or had strayed were restored and able to pour themselves into God's ministry and people again. A thousand or so pastors were so impacted that they wanted us to start a whole new movement. But we just wanted to serve them without overseeing something new. That's been our whole life, and I believe it's why people relate to us.

Beyond Bubble and Budget

Despite all the Lord's blessings, some people and groups still struggled with being in a multiracial setting that broke down barriers and accepted people as they were. The pastors' conferences reflected our church, and some attendees had never interacted with different races. It was hard to believe that anybody lived in that kind of bubble, but some people did.

At one conference we brought in a black pastor and his wife who were invited by black pastors they knew on our staff. They were good people but had been isolated in the black community and were skeptical of Tiz and me. Tiz introduced herself to the wife and gave her a big hug. As the week ended, she told Tiz that no white person had ever hugged her before—and she was forty-seven years old. Experiences like that make you realize what a difference you can make simply by being a friend to somebody.

When a prominent black pastor came and preached to us, he told me, "You need to show your congregation on television."

"Why?" I asked.

"Look at you," he said. "You're white, you're black, you're brown. How do you do that?"

"On purpose," I said. "We do it on purpose."

With that purpose comes a price. My good friend John Maxwell once told me, "You choose who you lose." Our stated intention has always been "This is our identity and our call. If this church doesn't suit you, that's OK. But for those who want to come along for the ride, this is how we roll."

We do what we do to break down the dividing walls and

build bridges instead. That requires the Lord's supernatural empowerment because we don't naturally have it in us. It takes courage to stand and not cave to the pressure, but the Holy Spirit within us is courageous. We take Joshua 1:9 to heart: "Be strong and of good courage; do not be afraid, nor be dismayed, for the LORD your God is with you wherever you go."

Believing that takes faith, but we've learned that the Lord is our source for everything we need. He is more dependable than any person, but people are often involved with His provision. We know He's faithful because He's come through for us again and again.

In everything He's directed us to do, He has been a trustworthy provider. It doesn't make sense, and the numbers don't always add up on the calculator. It's like the widow in the brutal famine who, in faith and obedience, prepared Elijah a meal with the last of her flour and oil. It made no sense in the natural, but her supply was miraculously replenished every day. "The jar of flour was not used up and the jug of oil did not run dry, in keeping with the word of the LORD spoken by Elijah" (1 Kings 17:16, NIV).

That is the story of our lives. Every time we act in faith and obedience, our cup is filled. The Lord continues providing resources and people to connect the dots and make things happen. God's part is His part, and then there's our part. We can't do His, and He won't do ours.

Portland is where we learned a new level of faith and enlarged our vision for what God could and wanted to do in our lives. In Portland we decided never to limit our God-given vision by our budget. If the Lord gave us the vision, we would pray in whatever we needed to accomplish His plan. This commitment took us to whole new levels of trusting the Lord, and He never let us down. As our church and outreach grew, so did the budget. We realized beyond any doubt that wherever God guides, He faithfully provides.

Going Global and Local

New Beginnings in Portland was also where we started to spread our wings globally. Doors swung open for miracle healing services worldwide and on a larger scale. We began doing radio broadcasts, which eventually led to television. Stepping into new arenas, we had to pray from a new level of faith, taking the limits off God and ourselves as our territory and influence expanded.

With television particularly, all the faith the Lord had developed in me since I was a saved junkie in Flagstaff came into play. Starting TV from scratch was a paradigm shift for our ministry. We'd been reaching people one-on-one through physical touch, but television sends out the Word through the airwaves. Our early productions were low-budget; a guy with a camera filmed them in a carved-out corner of our family room. The program first ran locally, but then the Lord connected us to larger platforms, and we ended up on TBN and Daystar.

I had just written the book *Free at Last: Breaking Generational Curses*. We could fill a library with testimonies from people who have been set free from generational curses through the years. One testimony involved a well-known minister and singer who came to New Beginnings. He was a great guy with a heavy anointing. Like me, he came out of a hard life of drugs. He asked to talk to me privately and said, "Larry, I know you came out of the same lifestyle as I did. Every day, I get up and have to fight the desire to do drugs again. Are you that way? Be honest with me."

"No, brother," I replied. "When I got set free, I got set free."

"You're kidding me," he said. "I've had to fight it for thirty years, every single day."

"No way, brother," I told him. "I need to pray with you and break the generational curse that's on your life."

This man was a minister, yet he said, "What are you talking about? The breaking of curses came with salvation. When you're saved, all that goes away."

I asked him some simple questions: "Then why do people still fight these things? Why do they fight the sin nature or a generational curse of poverty or failure? Why do they struggle with all those things?"

Christians *do* fight these battles. That's why we seek to learn more about the mysteries—to release the miracles so people can get free and enter all God has for them. I showed this man what the Scriptures said about breaking generational curses, and I gave him a copy of my book. We prayed together, and after thirty years of ministry, he was completely set free. He called me later, saying, "I can't believe it! Every day now, I wake up without that heaviness. The desire for drugs is gone. I fought this on my own all those years and didn't even know that God could set me free."

While in Portland, we also started to hold freedom break-through meetings. These weekend retreats focused on breaking generational curses, setting people free, and releasing each person onto a new course. When we went on TV with that teaching and book, everything took off because it ministered to so many people with wounds from their past. The message became a major thrust in what we taught and how we minis-tered, and it coincided with our developing global outreach.

We loved what was happening in Portland, and we planned to live there for the rest of our lives. After more than fifteen years, it was home. Our kids were well established and had

FROM JUNKIE TO JERUSALEM

deep, long-term friends. But change was coming, and adjustments would have to be made.

Burnt Out but Awakening

New Beginnings in Portland was bursting with growth, now running around the five-thousand mark and in the middle of revival. Tiz and I were doing television and writing books, and I was traveling a lot, speaking at conferences around the world and in the United States.

As exciting as it was, I was feeling burnt out—and it took a lot for me to reach that point. I preached multiple services on Sundays and was physically and emotionally exhausted. I was also shocked and grieved by some less-than-kosher business happenings behind the scenes at several prominent ministries I respected. My fatigue and disillusionment made me want to get out of the ministry. So I seriously thought about quitting—not on the Lord but on the ministry.

A friend from that time was a coinventor of the BowFlex machine. When it was first launched, he said, "You ought to buy some stock. This thing's going to be big." So we invested a few thousand dollars, and in two years it turned into about $13 million worth of stock. I thought I was set for life and seriously thought about leaving the ministry.

Then I heard God speak. He said, "You're a priest, not a king. Your job is ministry. You're spending too much time managing your finances." That was unexpected, but I knew it was God. I'd learned to recognize His voice, and He got my attention. So I refocused and hired a well-respected stockbroker in Portland to handle our affairs, particularly on this investment.

I was in the middle of writing a book called *10 Curses That Block the Blessing*. One of the curses involves racism and division. While researching, I discovered that the word *ghetto* was first used in Venice, Italy.[1]

This usage of the word *ghetto* was a surprise, because the word usually takes my mind to places like New York City or Los Angeles. So on the tail end of a ministry trip to Ukraine, Tiz and I took a side trip to Venice to do more research for the book. Turns out the word *ghetto* "comes from the Italian dialect form *ghèto*, meaning 'foundry.' A foundry for cannons was once located on an island that forms part of Venice, where in 1516 the Venetians restricted Jewish residence."[2] It essentially became a waste dump. In fact, the word *ghèto* is from *ghetàr*, which means to cast or throw.[3]

The terms *ghetto* and *gutter* can have related meanings.[4] I picture a gutter as an aluminum trough that runs around a roof and funnels water and debris. Our tour guide in Venice said the narrow streets actually functioned much that way. All the water, debris, and disease funneled down the streets of the ghetto, filling it with waste, sewage, and mud. That's where they confined the Jews. It must have been horrific. Through this research, however, the Lord brought me an awareness of what Jews have had to endure over the years.

As we were leaving Venice, our stockbroker called from Portland. "Listen," he said, "the stock market has crashed, and the only stock doing well is BowFlex. I know the company is making an announcement today on their reports. I think you ought to sell."

"Why sell?" I asked.

"I just have a feeling," he said.

Remember that God had told me, "Give this to a stockbroker to handle." Yet I told my stockbroker, "No. Don't even worry about it. I hear they are doing great."

"Larry," he urged, "I really think we ought to protect your gains."

"Don't worry about it," I reiterated, and Tiz and I boarded the plane.

By the time we landed in the States, the stock had crashed, and we lost $12 million overnight. "Riches certainly make themselves wings," wrote Solomon. "They fly away like an eagle toward heaven" (Prov. 23:5). My heart sank, and I felt a hollowness in the pit of my stomach. If only I'd listened. Yet even though I was bummed and still seriously considering leaving the ministry, God was up to something.

Tiz and I were good friends with a married couple in which the wife was from Israel. Knowing some of what we'd been going through, they asked, "Why don't you go to Israel with us?"

"Why would I want to go to Israel?" I replied.

"Just come. You'll enjoy it."

"Why not?" I answered. "I'm sure we'll have a good time." But in reality I had no interest at all in making the trip. All I wanted to do was be alone in the woods somewhere. Nevertheless, we traveled with them to Israel.

The visit was surprisingly refreshing and enlightening. We even met up with another friend of ours who is a Jewish pastor and a brilliant scholar who speaks nine languages. He accompanied us to Capernaum, where Jesus and Peter lived and where Jesus healed Peter's mother. Hundreds of tourists flock there annually, and most go straight to Jesus' and Peter's houses. But Joseph took us to the ancient synagogue where Jesus ministered. As we approached the front of the building, I noticed Hebrew writing around the stone doorframe and asked, "What's this?"

"Those are the names of some of the apostles' grandchildren," Joseph answered.

"Wait, wait, wait," I said. "The apostles' *grandchildren*? Were they not followers of Jesus?"

"Of course they were," he replied.

"But what were they doing in a synagogue?"

My scholar friend looked at me. "What are you talking about?" he asked and then paused, pondering his next words. "Larry, Jesus never came to start Christianity. His followers never called themselves Christians. Other people called them that. Jesus didn't come to start another religion; He came to graft us into the Jewish faith. They wrote the names of their grandchildren when they dedicated the synagogue. They were followers of the teachings of Rabbi Jesus."

There is a phenomenon in Israel called the Jerusalem syndrome. The disorder is "observed in tourists and pilgrims who visit Jerusalem" and suddenly identify themselves with and behave like biblical characters such as the apostles.[5] People who live in Israel know about this condition, and they watch for it in tourists.

As everyone else walked away, I stood there, taking in Joseph's words, and felt the presence of God come on me. At first I thought, "Is this syndrome thing happening to me?" Then the Lord spoke to me, saying, "I'm going to teach you to reread the Bible through the eyes of a Jewish Moses, a Jewish Abraham, a Jewish Jesus, and a Jewish Paul."

I didn't say anything to anybody until Tiz and I stood on our hotel balcony in Jerusalem, overlooking the Old City. Israel was celebrating their independence that day, and as the fireworks went off nearby, I told Tiz what had happened in Capernaum. I looked her in the eye and said, "I think we're about to start a new journey."

Tiz said, "What?"

I responded, "We're going to reread the Bible."

As my wife and I reread and studied the Bible through a new lens, our eyes opened to old life-changing truths, and we began falling in love with Israel. Then we began teaching what we learned about connecting our Christian teachings to our Judeo-Christian roots. It's been our most exciting, meaningful, and impactful journey so far.

Little did I realize the far-reaching impact of this experience.

The Derek Prince Anointing

Back in Portland, we continued holding our pastors' conferences. For one of them, we invited a pastor friend, who brought along a minister with a dynamic work in Colombia, South America. A group of us men went out to lunch. At the table the minister from Colombia, whom I'd never met and who spoke no English, said through an interpreter, "I had a dream last night, a vision. I don't know what it means, but I'm supposed to tell you."

"OK," I said.

"In the dream I was sitting on a platform with Derek Prince, and there was a sea of people coming to thank Derek for their deliverance and his teachings. Then we heard a roar behind us. Derek and I both turned, and a massive ocean of people was coming to be taught and delivered."

After taking a breath, the minister and his interpreter continued, "As Derek stood up and turned to the crowd, God's hand came out of heaven and rested on Derek. God said, 'Stay seated. I'm raising another.' I don't know what that means, but I was supposed to tell you."

"OK, this is bizarre," I said, "because I was a TV program last week. And the host [a prominent evangelist] said to me, 'You know something, Larry? Derek Prince's anointing is on you.'"

I continued to explain, "Not long after that, Tiz and I had lunch with a dear friend, who is like a mother in the Lord to us. We talked about my testimony and teaching on breaking generational curses, and our friend started to weep. I asked her if she was OK, and she said, 'Larry, Derek Prince's anointing is on you. His anointing is on you.' She knew nothing of what the TV evangelist had said. And though I have heard of Derek Prince, I don't know much about him."

My pastor friend looked at me across the table and declared, "You need to find Derek Prince. He's going to release his anointing on you. It's just like when Reinhard Bonnke was led to George Jeffreys' house in England and received his mantle."

"Well, I don't know anything about Derek Prince," I said.

One of the men commented, "I think he's living in Jerusalem."

"This is wild," I said. "I guess I'd better see what God is doing."

My friend had no idea how prophetic his words were. While we were still at the conference, our staff found Derek Prince's contact information and called his number. Derek's assistant answered, saying, "He's not receiving visitors right now, but may I ask why you're calling?"

They told the story, and the assistant said, "Stay by your phone. Let me get back to you." Five minutes later, he called back. "Derek said to come as soon as you can."

"When do you want us there?"

"You need to come as soon as possible," he urged.

We didn't know it at the time, but Derek was dying. We jumped on a plane to Jerusalem as soon as the conference ended. A member of Derek's team picked us up at the airport and took us directly to his home. When we walked in, his staff said, "We're so sorry. Derek is so weak that he can't get out of bed."

"We can go and come back later," I said.

"No, no, no. Derek said he believes God has kept him alive for this meeting."

We went into his room, which was barely big enough for his hospital bed. Derek was awake. I stood at his bedside with two of his men, and everybody else was in the doorway. "Tell me about yourself," Derek said with a weak and raspy voice.

After I told him my story and how I ended up in Jerusalem, he said, "I need to hear from God. Let's sing."

We began to sing and worship as the warm oil of God's presence filled the room in a way I had never experienced. As we basked in an attitude of worship, a very weakened Derek managed to say, "I've heard from God. Let me pray for you."

Derek could barely lift his arms, so I knelt beside him on the bed. Then suddenly his voice got strong, and he prophesied, "You will be the arrow shot from the bow in God's hands. And God says, 'I will shoot you to the nations of the world. And you will destroy the enemy that's trying to destroy My people.'"

Though more would be revealed about what that meant, I received the anointing and mantle Derek passed to me. I was so humbled and thought, "Who am I but an ex-junkie who is somehow, through everything, in Jerusalem receiving this anointing?" One of Derek's staff videoed the encounter. I've never shown it to anybody.

About an hour after we departed, his team called us and said, "Right after you left, Derek fell asleep, and he went home to be with the Lord."

Derek Prince believed that eventually the wall between the Jews and Gentiles would come down and that it would be a sign of the coming of the Messiah. From the very beginning of our ministry, Tiz and I went about breaking walls that divide, and we later learned about the power of breaking generational curses. We believe in seeing people set free, which is one of the reasons we're writing this book. Believe it or not, all this ties into understanding our Jewish roots and standing with Israel.

Recently, I was asked to open the prayer breakfast at the state Republican convention in Texas. The chaplain then invited me to come talk to their prayer group, commenting that Derek Prince had started the group. When I mentioned my Derek Prince story, he said, "We heard about that. That's why we want you to speak to us. You know, our prayer group is focused on two things. One is to pray for American politics, and the second is to pray for Israel and unity between Evangelicals and Israel."

This book is not only a testimony of what God can do with a nobody from the streets like me. It's also about unity and breaking down the walls that divide us in all the areas we've discussed, including with Israel. I believe it's one of the reasons God has entrusted us with this great mission at this point in history. A significant part of end-time prophecy is to unveil the understanding of Jewish roots and to bring Jews and Gentiles together.

Little did Tiz and I know on that day in Israel more than thirty years ago that we had stepped into the most important phase of our destiny. The trail of events since then has been astounding! Bible prophecy unfolds before our very eyes daily. Think about it. From the beginning of time, God saw the times that you and I are living in, and He saw us taking up the mantle to be part of His end-time prophecies.

This book is a testimony not just of our lives but also of God's call for you to be part of what He is doing. So get ready to hear more and be inspired about your own journey. Let God speak to His plans and His power in the world and in your life, family, and future!

Chapter 13

ANOINTED FOR ISRAEL

MY EXPERIENCE WITH Derek Prince in Jerusalem changed the course of our lives. And the chain of events leading up to that day was undeniably super-natural—first the evangelist's word about the Derek Prince anointing, then our friend's confirming word, and then the Colombian minister's confirming dream.

When the Lord sends a prophetic word, He often stamps His confirmations in threes. It's fitting that the third one came to me through a man from Colombia, the country where God saved my life when I cried out to Him. But God did not stop there. When my pastor friend said I had to find Derek Prince, I didn't know Derek was in Jerusalem or had dealings with Israel. Yet he was waiting in his Jerusalem bedroom, not feeling released to die until God sent me to him.

"You will be the arrow shot from the bow in God's hands," Derek prophesied. "And God says, 'I will shoot you to the nations of the world. And you will destroy the enemy that's trying to destroy My people.'" But what did that even mean? What would it look like as it played out?

I heard the words, but I knew I couldn't fulfill the prophecy on my own. I couldn't connect the dots or open the doors. Only the Lord could do that. I knew how flawed I was, and I knew what I had been—a junkie who, by all rights, should be dead or in jail.

Paul's words about himself resonate with me in so many ways: "I am the least of the apostles, who am not worthy to be called an apostle" (1 Cor. 15:9). If any particular anointing is given to me, it is a gift of grace. When the Lord does something like what He did with Derek Prince and me, it's for a reason. It is not because of any greatness of the vessels but only because of their willingness to be used.

I shared the encounter with Derek Prince only because it is critical to the story and to our ministry's view of Israel. My journey from the cocaine ranch to Jerusalem took more than fifty years, and I realize that I'm not the only arrow for Israel that the Lord is using. He has a quiver full, and each carries a specific anointing for a specific target.

My anointing is to help bring down the walls of division and build bridges through relationships of trust between Jews and Gentiles. How? By breaking the generational curse of anti-Semitism and replacement theology in the church world. This involves lovingly opening the eyes of both sides to the truths and mysteries of the Jewish roots that unlock the blessings and miracles of God, as we will see in the coming chapters. My point here is that when I was burnt out, discouraged, and wanting to quit the ministry, God ignited a fresh fire within my soul and readied me to be launched into this new phase.

At that time, the Portland church was a well-oiled machine, and it was cranking in a liberal city! It was amazing to see God moving in one of the most non-Christian regions of the country. Our staff, leaders, and congregation were fine-tuned in unity. People from all different backgrounds, races, and ages functioned as one in both purpose and actions.

We were so proud of that giant, loving family. Only God almighty could dial everybody in that way—and only through the Holy Spirit, who drew the people, joined their hearts, and transformed their lives. Jesus said, "No one can come to Me unless the Father who sent Me draws him" (John 6:44). Tiz and I and our family were simply willing vessels through which He flowed.

An Unexpected Nudge

In addition to the happenings in the Portland church, Tiz and I got into land development and real estate. It was mostly Tiz's venture. We learned to purchase big, empty fields, develop them, sell off the lots, and sometimes build homes and sell them too. The venture became profitable for us and enabled us to buy eighty acres to build our dream home.

We'd waited a long time to do this. So when we found property right across the Columbia River, we acted. The Mount Hood view, the deer and elk trails, the seven spring-fed streams, and a nearby crystal-clear lake were stunning. We loved riding horses through the woods to the Pacific Crest Trail. Life was good, and we felt like we were set.

Then one day I came home and told Tiz, "God put something on my heart."

Her eyebrows raised. "What's that?"

"I think God wants us to start another church."

She said, "Let me know how it goes."

"I'm serious, Tiz."

"But why would God want us to do that?"

Tiz had a point. It didn't make sense. The church was

bursting at the seams. We were debt-free and in the process of building a brand-new $12 million church building Our books and television ministry were taking off. Most importantly, lives were being changed. Still, something was stirring in my spirit. I remember sitting with several leading pastors and saying, "I feel like God wants me to start another church." Initially, I thought we would keep the church in Portland and branch out. I would preach at the new church one Sunday while Tiz would preach in Portland. Our plan was to alternate back and forth. Yet God was up to something bigger than us, and it would unfold as we followed the Holy Spirit's leading.

All the pastors I consulted with felt that Dallas was the best choice.

That made sense because TBN and Daystar were in Dallas, not to mention a huge population who needed our message of hope. As Tiz and I considered our move, TBN asked me to do a telethon out of their Houston studio. Tiz and I flew to Dallas, where she scouted the area for places to live while I did the telethon. I was about to go on air live when the station's manager ran into the studio and said, "Pastor Larry, phone call."

"I'm on in sixty seconds," I told her.

"It's Dr. Paul Crouch," she responded.

What could I say but "I guess I can be late"?

When I got on the line, Dr. Crouch asked, "Larry, am I hearing right? You're wanting to start a church in Dallas?"

"I think so," I said. "We're looking in Dallas."

He said, "We have a vacant building next to our studios that we use as a revival center. Why don't you take it? It seats three or four thousand."

"I appreciate the offer, Dr. Crouch, but we're going to pioneer. It's just Tiz and me. We can't afford that."

He said, "Don't worry about it. We'll make it work. God is in this."

I immediately called Tiz. She said, "You're not going to believe this, but I'm sitting in the TBN parking lot in Irving right now with the realtor saying this is the area we need to put our church!"

What a confirmation that God was leading us in this move! After His amazing provision, we announced on TV that we were holding an interest service in Dallas, and a thousand people came out. So in October 2004 we started New Beginnings Dallas. Within several months we nearly filled the big building in Irving.

Marcus, My Friend

Now that we were in Dallas, Joni and Marcus Lamb at Daystar frequently had us on their noontime show. Jan Crouch at TBN also had me come on the show she and Paul hosted to teach on the significance of the *tallit* (prayer shawl), touching the hem of Jesus' garment, and other significant truths from the Hebrew perspective.

For the Daystar program, Tiz and I typically joined Marcus and Joni on camera. Joni usually asked the questions while Marcus remained very quiet. But occasionally something would pique Marcus' interest, and he would say, "I've never heard that."

I remember a specific occasion when Marcus listened to my response and noted, "Joni, you and I both have Bible degrees. Why weren't we taught any of these things?" Then he turned to me and said, "Larry, we are doing a share-a-thon next week.

Why don't you come on and teach on the Jewish roots and standing with Israel?"

We did just that for one night, and the response was absolutely incredible. Overnight, Daystar's focus took a major shift toward supporting Israel. They grew to understand the importance of the issue and had a deep love for the Jewish people.

Marcus and I ended up becoming good friends and golfing buddies. We talked a lot about the importance of teaching the world about loving and blessing Israel. We both knew God brought us together in vision for such a time as this.

Then suddenly, on November 30, 2021, Marcus went to be with the Lord. He sent me a text message from his hospital room hours before he died. I was devastated to lose my dear friend. Within moments of his passing, my other closest friend, Owen Gann, also passed away. He had been with us from the beginning of the church in Portland and relocated to be with us in Dallas.

When these dear men died, I was truly heartbroken. Tiz and I would not be where we are today if not for Owen's friendship and support all those years. And we wouldn't be here without Marcus promoting the Israel message with us on Daystar. Owen was a quiet, shy man who hardly said a word but loved God and people and encouraged them one-on-one. Marcus was also an encourager, but his voice was heard around the world. Both men are receiving their eternal rewards, and both made a lasting impact that echoes to this day. What a lesson to us all! Every one of us in every walk of life has a mission, calling, and purpose in this world. God help us to fulfill our callings, our destinies, and His purposes.

Heretic

In Portland I taught about our Jewish roots for some time, and people experienced new levels of understanding, freedom, and blessings. Yet many leaders and churches labeled me a heretic. They claim that with the new covenant, God is basically done with the Jews and the church is the new Israel.

That's called *replacement theology.* Studying our Jewish roots highlights the error in that teaching and shows how Israel remains in God's plan. The Jews never stopped being His chosen people, and when Gentiles become born again, they are grafted into the olive tree that represents the Jews. (See Romans 11:11–31.)

I believe that appearing periodically on TBN and regularly on Daystar with Joni and Marcus (plus having our own program on Daystar) gave credibility and broad exposure to the truths we were teaching. Worldwide, eyes opened to God's current workings through Israel and the importance of our stand with them. This has been a global phenomenon, and I believe it is a fulfillment of Bible prophecy.

Malachi 4:6 says that in the end times, God "will turn the hearts of the fathers to the children, and the hearts of the children to their fathers." In Judaism much of what God says has an earthly meaning and a heavenly meaning—one physical and one spiritual. Physically, we believe that in the end times, the hearts of fathers and sons will be knitted together. Spiritually, however, the fathers in Malachi represent Israel, and the children represent the church. Those hearts will be knitted back together to usher in the coming of the Messiah.

This is playing out before our eyes as much of the church's viewpoint toward Israel has shifted. Jewish roots/Hebrew teaching and support for Israel are exploding, bringing Christians and

Jews together like never before. We've played a part in that, and our program on Daystar is among those that people most immediately respond to on Christian television. Something supernatural occurs in the hearts of the Father's children when they hear about Israel and how the Hebrew teachings bring both the Old and New Testament Scriptures to life.

Still the United Nations for Christ

After putting our ministry, church, congregation, Portland dream home, and land on the altar, Dallas became our new home. After sixteen years of pioneering and building relationships in Portland, we were looking forward to taking a breath and enjoying the fruit of our labor. But once again, the Lord was leading us to pick up, move on, and pioneer a new church.

This was our seventh time pioneering a church from the ground up, and we weren't those young, scrappy hippies anymore. We knew the labor and commitment involved in starting over again. Our kids were adults, and they also chose to uproot their lives, friendships, and security to make the move with us.

How amazing is that? As Tiz and I trusted God with our kids on all those pioneering missions, He was faithful to keep them. During our transition to Dallas, Anna and Brandin gave birth to twins, Luke and Jen got married, and Katie started her senior year of high school. It was not an easy time to uproot ourselves. Yet we did it, and a group of our staff pastors, families, and leaders did the same. Everyone had to dig in, adjust, and do whatever was necessary to start the Dallas church. I want to give credit and deep thanks to everyone who did that!

The church opened with nearly a thousand people who

followed our TV ministry, in a five-thousand-seat building—something few people get to do. It was all God's grace, and we received it while continuing the theme that we've taken into every city: We were determined to be the United Nations for Christ, reaching out to every walk of life and every background, every side of the tracks, every color, and every nationality, so we could all serve God together. And just like our church plants in other cities, we broke down those racial divides. There were large, powerful white churches and large, powerful black churches in Dallas. But not many crossed over. We faced criticism and obstacles from both sides, yet we chose to stay true to our calling.

This time we were growing a church in the Bible Belt, which was a new, eye-opening experience. In addition to the usual racial and economic barriers, we faced many traditions and religious doctrines, especially regarding women in leadership and women as teachers. We even got kicked off a radio station when they discovered that Tiz also teaches and preaches.

Today, New Beginnings Dallas is approximately one-third white, one-third black, and one-third Hispanic, with smaller numbers of Asians and Native Americans in the mix. Being multicultural is what we're about, along with our Jewish roots and stand for Israel. God told Abram, "I will bless those who bless you, and I will curse him who curses you; and in you *all* the families of the earth shall be blessed" (Gen. 12:3, emphasis added). As it does in Romans 8:28, *all* means "all." People of all races and economic levels are blessed when they support Israel. And we believe that our being a United Nations for Christ plays into God's entrusting us with building bridges between the Jewish community and Christianity.

It is never easy to leave a city, but we knew that leaving Portland was a God thing. It was certainly not easy on any of my family or in any way. Starting over is incredibly challenging, stressful, and exhausting. Leaving so many good friends and a thriving church behind was heart-wrenching to us all, but we were convinced God had led us to Dallas.

As I said, we thought we would be pastoring both churches and commuting back and forth. However, not everything turned out exactly as we envisioned. Some of the leaders who took the reins in Portland led the church toward their own vision and direction. For those who wanted to continue with mine and Tiz's vision, we started live streaming our Sunday services from Dallas into a hotel ballroom in Portland. The live streamers there continue to be very involved with what we're doing. They're givers and tithers, and they support New Beginnings' projects. They are very community-minded, and they all know and love each other.

The pastors in that group shepherd the people and host the service as an extension of New Beginnings' vision and voice. We also visit periodically to minister in person. Some of the people in the streaming service have assimilated into other churches while remaining part of New Beginnings. We're all letting the Holy Spirit guide us in new and creative ways to get the message out.

Today, we have thousands of live stream partners and viewers all over the world. It's amazing! In addition, Tiz and I have a daily TV program called *New Beginnings with Larry and Tiz Huch* that reaches nearly the entire world. It is an incredible honor to have hundreds of thousands of people partnering with us to support and bless Israel.

Our church in Dallas is a thriving, vibrant, multicultural, multiracial mixture of people from every age group and walk of life. We have ministries for kids, youth, young adults, prime timers, and life groups to build relationships and help meet the needs of people. We're loving, accepting, growing, on fire, and a lively bunch that love God, love people, and love helping others in need. We teach our people that "we are blessed to *be* a blessing." And they certainly strive to live that way. Our church is very supportive of and a great blessing to Israel.

We have an incredible congregation that we love dearly and are very proud of. Our kids are all on staff and/or in leadership. When we came to Dallas, God gave Tiz the promise that He would give us people for our lives (Isa. 43:4). And He certainly has done that!

The Blessing Continues

Several years after our move to Dallas, the Lord miraculously opened an opportunity to buy our own building in Bedford, a Dallas suburb. The vacant structure was a condemned 1980s theater complex with broken windows, bad wiring and plumbing, water damage, and a caving roof. Tiz and I looked past all the mess and envisioned an excellent church facility. We began remodeling and restoring the building and turned it into an incredible modern sanctuary, well-equipped for large events and fellowship. We even created an amazing youth wing called Kid City, complete with a big playscape and a train to take kids for rides outside.

The building's story resonates with the stories of so many people we've reached over the decades. God restores not only condemned and abandoned buildings but also lives. He miraculously breathes into them His life, beauty, and joy. He fixes broken hearts and our broken world because He is in the restoration business. For Tiz and me, one of the greatest joys is seeing people from all the churches and ministries we've served over the years who have been restored by God and who live wonderful, productive lives. Because of His touch they are building great families, businesses, and ministries and impacting other people.

If that weren't blessing enough, God has graced our ministry and people so much that we have been debt-free for more than ten years. Instead of managing mortgages we can focus on expanding our vision, outreach, and influence for the Lord. Our church is thriving and growing! Our daily TV program reaches every corner of the world. And we are incredibly privileged to participate in something we will talk more about: *tikkun olam*,[1] or repairing a broken world.

Chapter 14

JOURNEY OF DESTINY

OSEA 4:6 SAYS, "My people are destroyed for lack of knowledge," but Jesus offers us hope, saying, "You shall know the truth, and the truth shall make you free" (John 8:32). Knowledge of the truth brings freedom! My journey of falling in love with our Jewish roots, with the land of Israel, and with the people of Israel has made me freer. It is truly a journey of destiny.

As you know, the Lord spoke to my heart in Capernaum, saying, "I'm going to teach you to reread the Bible through the eyes of a Jewish Moses, a Jewish Abraham, a Jewish Jesus, and a Jewish Paul." With the knowledge I gleaned came the birth of an additional calling and direction. The Lord sharpened the tip of the arrow before He shot it!

As God reconnected me to the Jewish roots of our faith, I discovered "hidden secrets" in His Word—revelations that have accidentally or intentionally been lost in translation. As Paul explained, "We speak wisdom among those who are mature, yet not the wisdom of this age, nor of the rulers of this age, who are coming to nothing. But we speak the wisdom of God in a mystery, the hidden wisdom which God ordained before the ages for our glory" (1 Cor. 2:6–7).

Steps in the Journey

Step 1

The journey into studying our Jewish roots started simply for Tiz and me. The first step was to realize that Jesus didn't speak English or Greek; He likely spoke Aramaic, an ancient language similar to Hebrew. So whenever I studied a subject, whether for personal edification or in preparation for teaching, I went to the Hebrew rather than the Greek. It sounds so simple now, but it was the beginning of a major shift in my life and ministry. What did being baptized mean in the language of Jesus? What did it mean when the woman touched the hem of His garment? What does it mean that the festivals are "a shadow of things to come" (Col. 2:17)?

The Bible often speaks about having eyes but not seeing and having ears but not hearing. As a pastor who has always loved studying the Word, I suddenly found my eyes and ears opening to things that I'd heard and taught for years. I realized that although I knew of these things, I had missed what the Lord was actually saying.

For instance, Jesus often said, "It is written," but what was He referencing? The obvious answer is the Word of God, but let's think about that. The New Testament had not yet been written. So Jesus was referring to the Old Testament, including the Torah, the first five books. I missed out on so much of the depth, true meaning, and power of what Jesus said. He referred to Old Testament passages from Deuteronomy, Psalms, Isaiah, and other books, which means He taught as a Jewish rabbi.

Of course, everyone knows that Jesus was Jewish. But

discovering that Jesus was born a Jew, lived as a Jew, practiced the Jewish faith, and taught as a Jewish rabbi out of the ancient Torah was life-altering to me. The teachings of Jesus that Christianity is based upon were predominantly teachings straight out of Judaism and the Old Testament. He wasn't starting a new religion of His own. He didn't ask people to become "Christians." He asked them to follow God's existing teachings, to bring them back to God in their hearts and lives. The term *Christianity* was labeled later as a reference to those who followed Him, Jesus Christ. This was the key to unveiling the mysteries of God's Word.

Let me explain. If someone said, "I saw Pastor Larry riding a thousand-pound hog," you could interpret that a couple of ways. When some hear the word *hog*, they think of a pig. But if you're from South St. Louis, a hog is a Harley-Davidson. It's a matter of listening with the right filter or seeing with the right lens. We must see the Bible through the lens of the Jewish people's eyes and thinking.

Step 2

The second step in exploring our Jewish roots was to connect what I read in the New Testament with what was taught in the Old Testament. I had to discover what scholars and rabbis taught and the wisdom that came from ancient Jewish perspectives. Seeking ancient Jewish wisdom was my stepping stone into the next part of my journey of destiny.

Step 3

The third step in understanding our Jewish roots was to recognize that we are called by God to prepare the world for the coming of the Messiah. But how? The answer is in understanding the "one new man" in Ephesians 2:15. This is about spiritually building the tabernacle of David and breaking down the dividing wall between Jews and Gentiles. It's called *unity*. Where there is unity, God commands His blessing. (See Psalm 133.) I saw that for God's people to be blessed, we must be united, not divided.

Did you know that in the tabernacle of David, no wall of division separated Jews and Gentiles? Therefore, God could move among the people with a great spiritual outpouring. He wants to do this today with signs, wonders, and miracles. Studying Ephesians 2:19–22 with a new lens opened my eyes to the wisdom of God's Word and truth from both the New Testament apostles and the Old Testament prophets. Ephesians 2:19–20 talks about the "household of God" being "built on the foundation of the apostles and prophets." When we add their wisdom to our faith, we tear down the walls of division, and the two (Jews and Gentiles) become one.

Step 4

The fourth step in our Jewish roots journey was to focus on repairing the breach that exists between Christians and Jews so we become a unified "dwelling place of God in the Spirit." (See Ephesians 2:21–22.) We need to repair the damage that has been done to the Jewish people, mainly by the church, over the past two thousand years. It took years before the Jewish community would trust me in this. Think about the Crusades, torture, exile, and hatred, not to mention the Holocaust, that the Jewish world has suffered because of false teaching in the church—from blaming the Jews for killing Jesus to lies and fabrications about the Jewish people and culture to ridiculous fearmongering that the Jews are trying to rule the world.

Even in our tumultuous times, anti-Semitism has erupted with claims that Jews are trying to commit genocide against the

Palestinian people. People who make these claims want us to believe that the Jews are "occupiers" of Palestine/Israel. (I will explain this much further and deeper in an upcoming chapter.) From the beginning of this journey till today, Tiz and I regularly meet Jewish people and tell them our story about loving and supporting Israel. Most of the time they are astounded. "What?" they say. "You are Christian pastors, and you love Israel and the Jewish people? We thought you hated us."

A formidable wall has divided Christians and Jews for thousands of years, and tearing it down is a big job. Thankfully, we serve a bigger God. This mission fulfills an end-time biblical prophecy that is playing out before us as we watch the news. We are living in the most exciting times in all history, and we get to be a part of it!

God's First Promise with a Blessing

In Judaism, Genesis 12:3 is referred to as the father of all blessings. This is the foundational truth of understanding our biblical Jewish roots.

> I will bless those who bless you, and I will curse him who curses you; and in you all the families of the earth shall be blessed.

Learning, understanding, and practicing this is what guides the direction of our entire life and ministry. It's the most important thing I can teach you to enter into God's promises and blessings. Without a doubt, I know that the miracles and blessings in my life and family are a direct result of this.

So how do we begin to tear down the walls and restore the breach between Christians and Jews? By loving one another. The Hebrew term *tikkun olam* means to repair or mend a broken world. It refers to improving both the physical and spiritual world through compassion, social justice, charity, and acts of kindness.[1] It comes directly from the Talmud and is considered a central concept of Judaism. God made it clear that He was leading me not only to learn from my Jewish brothers and sisters but to *tikkun olam* in any way I could.

The whole idea of making the world a better place became huge for Tiz and me, but it's for all of us. God wants to change the world, starting with our families and circles of influence. Everyone can impact others by *tikkun olam,* even if one's circle consists of only one other person.

I found in my study of ancient Jewish wisdom that everything God teaches has two sides, spiritual and physical, heavenly and earthly. We started looking for ways to bless the people and land of Israel. We began by blessing Holocaust survivors with financial support, food, and supplies. Partnering with a prominent Israeli hospital, we built an emergency trauma wing and provided other types of medical support. We supported a marvelous children's home, along with specific programs that help children deal with the post-traumatic stress caused by terrorist bombings. Because the children's home is only twelve seconds away from impact when rockets are fired from Lebanon, we've also built more than twenty bomb shelters in Israel.

We truly believe what Matthew 6:33 says: "Seek first the kingdom of God and His righteousness, and all these things shall be added to you." We are to *seek* righteousness, as in looking for a hidden treasure. Obviously that involves living righteous and holy lives, which is the spiritual or the heavenly part. But the word *righteous* in Hebrew is *tzedakah*, which can refer to kindness, acts of charity, and good deeds.[2] This is the earthly application of righteousness. Righteousness is about not only the condition of the heart but also what we do to help and bless people.

I've been to Israel forty-eight times. Just this morning, I called to check on a friend who's in Israel. As of this writing, the nation has been at war for more than a year, following the October 7, 2023, massacre by Hamas. At the end of the conversation with my friend, I asked what the needs are and what we can do to help. Whether we're calling or visiting Israel, we *are seeking* where we can help with acts of kindness and charity. We are *seeking* ways to tear down the two-thousand-year-old wall of division. We are searching for ways to repair the breach.

One of the needs we support involves *aliyah*—the return of Jews to Israel from all over the world. *Aliyah* is a Hebrew word meaning "elevation" or "going up."[3] I knew that a major theme in Old Testament prophecy involved the miraculous gathering of the Jews from the four corners of the earth to return to the Promised Land. (See Isaiah 11:12 and 43:5–6, for example.) Then I discovered that Gentiles and Christians were to partner with God and Israel to make it happen. Isaiah 49:22 declares, "Thus says the Lord GOD: 'Behold, I will lift My hand in an oath to the nations, and set up My standard for the peoples; they shall bring your sons in their arms, and your daughters shall be carried on their shoulders.'"

When Russia attacked Ukraine a couple of years ago, I immediately called to ask friends in Israel's government what we could do for Ukraine's Jews. People in our church and around the world responded that very day and made a huge impact. We couldn't mention it then, but in addition to getting our Jewish brothers and sisters out of Ukraine, we helped many Russian Jews make *aliyah*!

We understand that the Bible's first promise with blessing is Genesis 12:3 (which says that blessings come to those who bless Israel). In Hebrew this is called the *Avos* or *Avot*, the father of all blessings.[4] When commandments, instructions, or lists appear in God's Word, the first thing is the foundation and the most important. The fulfillment of everything else coming after it depends on the first item in the top priority. Judaism teaches that how a thing ends is determined by how it begins. Tiz likes to illustrate this by saying the Avos is the top button. If you don't get your top button right, nothing else lines up. Get the top button right and everything does line up.

As an example, Ephesians 6:11–18 talks about putting on the whole armor of God so that you can defeat the enemy. The first item in the armor appears in verse 14, where God speaks of "having your loins girt about with truth" (KJV). Loins are designed to reproduce life. The key to resisting the enemy (whose domain is death) is to first know the truth.

Where the Jewish Jesus is concerned, nothing works in the absence of truth. Notice also that the second piece of the armor is the breastplate of righteousness (v. 14). Remember that righteousness includes acts of charity and kindness.

Genesis 12:3 is the *Avos* or *Avot*, the father of every promise of God and the key to end-time signs, wonders, and miracles. Through Israel and the Jewish people, all the world has been blessed. Therefore, our desire to bless them has been a natural step in our journey. We continually look for opportunities to encourage and bless Israel. But I must admit, we've seen an amazing bonus.

Let me explain. For more than thirty years, we have supported Israel. Our daily TV program teaches about Christianity's Jewish roots and involves praying for Jerusalem's peace, repairing the breach, and showing the Jewish people that we love them. We have asked people worldwide to help us by supporting Holocaust survivors, children's homes, bomb shelters, *aliyah*, ambulances that serve as mobile ICU units, and so many other lifesaving and life-changing projects.

So what is the bonus I mentioned? It is stated in Matthew 6:21: "Where your treasure is, there your heart will be also." God has given us a strategy for sharing with the world the needs of Israel and the Jewish people as they face anti-Semitism. As a result, many escape and fulfill Bible prophecy by making *aliyah* and settling in the land God promised to the Jewish people. The amazing bonus is that as people put their treasures (or finances) into Israel, their hearts also return to Israel, and the wall of division is eroded. We have seen this happen in huge ways. Those walls will come down!

Step 5

When I started this journey of destiny, I didn't know it would lead to a fifth step. I almost wrote "the final step," but the Holy Spirit stopped me and said the fifth step is not the last one. But it reminds me of what David wrote in Psalm 37:23 about the steps of a righteous man being ordered or guided by the Lord.

Due to our commitment to Israel, Tiz and I have been greatly honored to meet spiritual and political (heavenly and earthly) leaders from around the world. In Jerusalem a few years ago, friends from Israel's government invited me to a special dinner where about eleven hundred of Israel's largest Jewish donors were to meet. I was seated at a table toward the back of the room with the only other Gentile or Christian in the room. It was a great night, and I met some wonderful people. Everyone was disappointed to learn, however, that due to the escalation of violence at Israel's northern border, Prime Minister Netanyahu would be unable to attend.

Nevertheless, the banquet went on. After several speeches,

dinner, and the giving of awards and appreciation, a large number of military men entered the room and roped off a section. When they turned to stand guard, in walked the prime minister to a loud, joyous standing ovation. We were all ecstatic, but he looked weary. He gave a brief, encouraging speech and then sat down at a table with his wife and other Israeli leaders. Everyone tried to get cell phone photos of Mr. Netanyahu by leaning over the guards' rope.

As my team and I sat in the back watching, a woman who was sitting with the prime minister and his wife rose from their table, ducked under the rope, and walked past the guards, through the crowd, and all the way back to our table. "Pastor Larry," she said, "the prime minister would like to say hello to you."

When she escorted me to his table, Prime Minister Netanyahu looked me in the eye and said, "Pastor Larry, I watch your TV program whenever I can. I want to thank you for all you do and say for Israel. Keep up the good work."

Then Mrs. Netanyahu said, "Pastor, I watch you every day too. I love what you're doing for Israel."

I was amazed to learn that these two great people cared about what a guy from the South St. Louis streets had to say. I was even more blessed to know that we were making a difference in the world.

During another visit to Jerusalem, I received an unexpected telephone invitation. The caller said, "Pastor Larry, Mr. Herzog would like to meet with you tomorrow for breakfast." Isaac Herzog was soon to be the president of Israel and remains in that position today. (Israel is a parliamentary democracy that has both a president who serves as the head of state and a prime minister who holds executive power.)

When I entered the room to meet Mr. Herzog, I was beyond shocked and honored. He put out his hand and said, "I wanted to meet the pastor who is not trying to convert us but telling the world to love us."

Never in my wildest dreams could I have imagined the political and spiritual steps God would lead me through after my momentous first trip to Israel. Since seeing the names of the apostles' grandchildren scribbled in Hebrew above the synagogue doors, I have been privileged to share the truth about Israel every day via worldwide TV—with Tiz and now with our daughter Katie. As I write this chapter, Katie and I are preparing to leave for Bangkok, Singapore, and Hong Kong, where we will speak to leaders on behalf of Israel. It's mind-boggling to see God using our lives and voices the way He does!

Remember that God promised the Jewish people that He would give them land—not only to them but to their descendants *forever*. (See Genesis 13:15.) Why are they called Jews and not West Bankers? Because they are from the region of Judah and Samaria—the land of Ju-dea!

Our journey of destiny has taken us from the simple study of the Bible's Hebrew words to a political understanding of the ancient land. I have learned that you can't separate the spiritual from the political. In Genesis 13:15, God told Abram, "All the land which you see I give to you and your descendants forever." It's an everlasting covenant. (See also Genesis 12:7.) As Psalm 105:8–11 explains, "He remembers His covenant forever, the word which He commanded, for a thousand generations, the covenant which He made with Abraham, and His oath to Isaac, and confirmed it to Jacob for a statute, *to Israel* as an everlasting covenant, saying, 'To you I will give the land of Canaan as the allotment of your inheritance'" (emphasis added).

I wonder, is it political or spiritual to tell the historical truth of the land called Israel? The name Jerusalem is mentioned more than eight hundred times in Scripture but not even once in the Quran.[5] Where did the name Palestine come from? The Roman emperor Hadrian gave the region this name after the Bar Kokhba Revolt in AD 132.[6] The Roman government was obsessed with destroying and conquering the Jews and was frustrated by their resilience and relentless spirit. Out of spite, they renamed the land after Israel's ancient enemies, the Philistines. Remember that Islam didn't even begin until AD 610.[7]

We can show that from 1517 to December 1917 all the land was under Ottoman rule, which was largely Turkish.[8] In November 1917 a letter from Britain's foreign secretary called for "the establishment in Palestine [Israel] of a national home for the Jewish people." This letter came to be known as the Balfour Declaration.[9] Then in 1920, at the San Remo conference after World War I, the Allies passed mandates for the administration of three former Ottoman territories in the Middle East: Syria, Mesopotamia, and Palestine (Israel). Under these mandates, the "individual countries were deemed independent but subject to a mandatory power until they reached political maturity."[10] Please note that when historical references are made to the country of Palestine, it refers not to a nation of the Palestinian people but to the nation of Israel.

In 1948 Israel was officially recognized by the world as an independent, sovereign Jewish nation. Long before this, however, history and the Bible proved that Israel was the Jewish homeland. There has never been a Palestinian state or government. The terrorist Yasser Arafat simply "announced the establishment of an independent Palestinian state (without defined borders)"[11] and became chairman of the Palestine Liberation Organization, which professed to represent Palestinians worldwide.[12] I could go on from a biblical, historical, and political standpoint about the history of the Jews and their right to exist and live in Israel, but that is a conversation for another time.

My point here is that the first step in my destiny journey resulted from wanting to better understand God's Word and teach our church how to live in His blessings, promises, and miracles. However, the Lord knew that was only the beginning! Because of my studies and teachings on connecting, I was asked to be on the executive board of the Israel Allies Foundation (based in Jerusalem and Washington, DC), which is involved in faith-based diplomacy, a concept fathered by Josh Reinstein.[13]

Formed in 2004, the Israel Allies Foundation (IAF) was one of the first political organizations to unite Jews and Christians to stand for Israel. We build relationships with government leaders, teaching them why it's so important biblically, politically, and historically to stand with Israel. We have been instrumental in passing legislation in many nations that impact Israel. We also helped with the policies that President Trump courageously undertook (which no other president dared to do), such as moving the American embassy from Tel Aviv to Jerusalem. This important move made an international statement; it said that America recognizes Jerusalem as the capital of Israel. This is huge!

In addition, I was invited to be in Jerusalem by Josh Reinstein, president of IAF, when President Trump went on his first presidential visit to Israel. After he and Prime Minister Netanyahu spoke in Jerusalem, some of us were asked to stay and have a picture taken with both these great men and their wives. We were accompanied by a security escort and were ushered out immediately after the photo was taken, but not before I was granted a quick handshake with both leaders, a "God bless you," and another photo. As I walked away, I felt someone grab my arm from behind. It was the prime minister, who thanked me again for standing with Israel. Both he and his lovely wife reiterated their appreciation for our TV program and the difference our ministry was making. It was an amazing, wonderful day for me and an incredible honor!

Another special connection has formed with Ron Dermer, who currently serves as Israel's minister of strategic affairs. He has become a great friend over the years, partly through our work with Sam Grundwerg, the world chairman of Keren Hayesod (United Israel Appeal). Sam is one of my very best friends in the world. Both Ron and Sam have been guest speakers at New Beginnings in Dallas, and I was able to host them at a Dallas Cowboys game in the private suite of another great friend.

In a very exciting moment, with Dallas on the goal line and about to win the game, Ron said, "Pastor Larry, I have a phone call for you."

I said, "Ron, we're about to score. Can't it wait?"

He responded, "You really should take this call."

When I answered the phone, I immediately recognized the voice on the other end as Prime Minister Netanyahu's.

"Mr. Prime Minister, hello!" I exclaimed.

"Pastor Larry," he said, "I heard you were with Ron and Sam. I just want to say thank you once again from myself and the people of Israel. We appreciate all you do for us. Keep up the good work!"

That was a highlight of my life, as was being with President Trump on several occasions. I regard these men highly. When either man enters a room, the atmosphere instantly becomes calm. It's like, "OK, Dad is here now." It's the feeling that God's leaders are present and that everything will be all right.

There are so many other leaders I have met and greatly respect. One is Texas senator Ted Cruz. The other is the former United States ambassador to Israel, David Friedman, who works tirelessly on behalf of the nation and people of Israel. Both are great men of God and, I'm proud to say, good friends.

It Is Spiritual Too

You might think that I've gotten off track here, starting out on a spiritual journey with Israel but seeming to end up in politics. But remember that everything God does is both spiritual and physical, heavenly and earthly, so I will bring the other part of the story into focus.

A few years ago the Keren Hayesod organization gave me the first-ever John Henry Patterson Guardian of Zion Award to honor the work that we do for Israel.[14] Patterson was a British army lieutenant colonel who commanded the Jewish Legion (which served as the foundation of the Israeli defense force, or IDF, decades later) during World War I. As a Christian, an advocate, and a friend to Israel, Patterson was influential in many decisions that impacted Israel's becoming a nation in 1948—so much so that Prime Minister Netanyahu's brother Yonatan was named after him.[15] Patterson courageously devoted his military and civilian life to fighting anti-Semitism, so to have the Israeli government create an award for me named after John Patterson is an honor beyond my wildest dreams.

When we went to Jerusalem to receive the award, I was asked whether I'd like to visit Prime Minister Netanyahu or President Herzog. Of course I said, "Either one, but I would also love to meet Rabbi **Meir Lau**."

Sam Grundwerg had given me a book by the rabbi titled *Out of the Depths*. It describes the rabbi's journey of destiny from surviving the Holocaust death camps to becoming the chief rabbi of Israel. What an amazing story and courageous man! When I mentioned that I wanted to meet him, everyone was less than enthusiastic and said he probably would not care to meet with a Christian pastor. I totally understood, especially after reading his story and what he and so many other Jews had suffered at the hands of so-called Christians.

To my surprise, I learned the next day that we were going to Rabbi Lau's house. We were granted five minutes to meet with him; then we'd have to leave, as he was preparing for Shabbat. However, our five minutes stretched to twenty minutes. After we talked and studied the Torah together, Rabbi Lau pulled me aside and asked, "Pastor, how do you know all these things?"

I told him that God had led me to study the Torah from the Hebrew. I can still feel his eyes and heart as he held my hand and said, "That's because of the Jewish roots of Christianity."

"Yes sir, Rabbi," I replied. "I believe that with all my heart."

Then Rabbi Lau gave me a big hug and said, "That's because Jesus never stopped being Jewish."

That was exactly what God had shown and taught me! I was so blown away by the rabbi's understanding of this that I almost couldn't respond. "No sir, He didn't," I finally said. "And Rabbi, with God's help, that's what I'm trying to teach the world."

He asked, "Pastor, what are you doing in April?"

"What do you want me to be doing in April, Rabbi?" I answered.

"Walk with me in the March of the Living," he said. "Let's show the world a rabbi and a pastor walking together in unity."

The March of the Living consists of thousands of Jews who walk from Auschwitz to Birkenau every year to honor the six million Jews murdered in the Holocaust.[16] I accepted his invitation, and we did the next march together—a rabbi and a pastor in solidarity, showing the world that Jews and Christians agree: "Never again."

In 2024, my team and my family attended the March of the Living again, for the first time since the October 7, 2023, massacre. We walked, sat, and stood with Rabbi Lau in solidarity and defiance of the atrocities that the world has brought against the Jewish people and the nation of Israel. We will continue to be a voice, a light, and a people who stand as Jews and Christians telling the world, "Never again." You might ask, "Is this journey from junkie to Jerusalem spiritual or political?" For all of us, it is a historical journey orchestrated and destined by God Himself. I can't wait to see what's next!

I'm excited to hear about what God is birthing and forming in your life, family, and future! You too can leave behind your past and limitations and step into a new beginning and future filled with God's promises and blessings. The Lord wants to use your life to make impact in the world for Him and for good. What He has done for me He can do for you. God took my journey from "once a junkie, always a junkie" to Jerusalem, allowing me to tell and show the people of Israel and Jews around the world that God loves them and that we, as Christians, love them too.

My calendar is packed with trips to countries that want to support, understand, and be linked to the nation and people of Israel. For the past two years, I've spoken at the March for Jesus in Brazil, where around two million people march through the streets to celebrate and honor Jesus. The March for Jesus now celebrates and honors Israel![17] It is a phenomenon and a miracle!

The Lord is doing great things across the world, and all of us can be a vital part of it. What an exciting honor—and we're just getting started!

Chapter 15

GOD IS BIGGER THAN YOUR DIAGNOSIS

W HEN GOD MAKES a promise, you can take it to the bank. He said that when you bless Israel, He will bless you and be personally involved in your life. In May 2018, our team and I were in Israel with Ambassador Friedman when the United States moved its embassy from Tel Aviv to Jerusalem. We were privileged to be part of the events, including the celebratory dinner afterward.

The day after the celebration, several friends and I were on Ben Yehuda Street eating New York–style pizza when my friend's phone rang. His wife was calling from Washington, DC. After a couple of seconds, he told her, "Well, he's right here," and he handed me the phone.

"Pastor," she said with some urgency in her voice, "I had to call you. God told me to call you right now, at this moment. It couldn't wait till tomorrow. I don't know why, but God told me to tell you that the lion will roar from Jerusalem, and the roar will be heard around the world."

Being in Jerusalem for a momentous occasion, I thought maybe the message was related to Israel. Still, the urgency of the message seemed odd. I said, "Thank you," and handed the phone back to my friend.

When I shared the conversation with my friends, we all assumed it had something to do with the Lion of Judah, who was going to roar from Jerusalem. The phrase *Lion of Judah* comes out of the Book of Revelation: "Do not weep. Behold, the Lion of the tribe of Judah, the Root of David, has prevailed to open the scroll and loose its seven seals" (5:5).

Two minutes later, however, my phone rang. It was my son, Luke, and my daughter-in-law, Jen. They sounded upset, and Luke said, "Dad, Lion is really sick, and we're taking him to the hospital."

My grandson Lion was seven months old at the time. In light of my son's call, the timing of my friend's wife's message seemed uncannily prophetic. I made it a priority to get home as quickly as I could.

Sure enough, our little Lion was very sick. A couple of weeks of testing confirmed that he had a rare form of leukemia. The doctor gave us a dark, gloomy prognosis. He told us that he could not find reports of a single infant who survived this type of leukemia. My family and I were devastated, and we struggled to wrap our minds around the news. Instinctively, however, we shifted into prayer-and-faith mode. We declared God's promises of divine healing over Lion and claimed the promise of blessing from Genesis 12:3.

Listen closely and hear me on this. When God says, "I will bless those who bless you and curse those who curse you," pay attention. He's talking about Israel, and the words are not coming from a preacher or evangelist who might exaggerate. They are coming from God Himself.

We contacted everyone we knew and alerted them to Lion's plight. Rabbis and our Jewish friends in Israel prayed for us in their synagogues and at the Western Wall. Our church, along with friends and family from across the nation, prayed. Partners from our live stream and TV show interceded for us, as did churches and ministries around the world.

God heard all those prayers. He had plans for Lion, and they weren't plans for leukemia. There were great miracles ahead! Against all odds, Lion kept getting better. That was seven years ago now, and Lion is just finishing first grade as I write this chapter. He is cancer free. It's an absolute miracle, proving that God is bigger than your diagnosis!

More Devastating News

Not long after the news that Lion was sick and embarking on his healing journey, Tiz and I were back in Israel. One morning she said, "You know, I'm not feeling very well."

When we got home, she still didn't feel up to par, so she went to the doctor. After running some initial tests, the doctor referred her to an oncologist. Tiz and I and our girls, Katie and Anna, went to the oncologist's office together, where he gave us the diagnosis: ovarian cancer, and it was quite advanced. He said Tiz probably had it for only a month or two, but it was moving fast. He continued, "I've opened up my schedule, and I will operate in three days. Then we'll do chemo for six months. If we don't take these steps, you probably won't have three months to live. If we do them, we can hope for your condition to improve, but with cancer there are no guarantees."

Tiz's oncologist is a wonderful doctor, and we did all that he told us to do. But we also believed that God was bigger than the cancer and the statistics.

So once again desperate prayers from our friends all over the world, Jews and Christians, poured out, and God showed

Himself bigger than this horrific diagnosis. Against all odds, Tiz's condition did not deteriorate. She just kept getting better, amazing the medical community. That was also six years ago as of this writing. But about one year ago, Tiz had a relapse and got extremely sick.

She dropped thirty-five pounds in a couple of months. Her doctors in Dallas said, "This is what happens at the end. There's nothing left that we can do. Your body is just shutting down." We were shocked but again pressed in to faith and prayer and believed God had another answer—a miracle.

Within a few days, a great friend of ours, who is the CEO of a major home improvement chain, found out about Tiz and contacted me. He had contacts at a leading cancer hospital in Los Angeles and insisted that we had to get her there right away.

He made a call to get Tiz an appointment, and she and Katie flew out there two days later. She saw a leading oncologist and surgeon, and they immediately scheduled her for surgery and subsequent treatment.

Five days after the surgery a leading member of the medical team came to Tiz's hospital room and told her, "You probably had only weeks or days to live."

"Well, you guys saved my life," Tiz responded.

You know what the doctor said? "No. We didn't. In this case only God could have done that."

Six months later Tiz is alive, healthy, and strong. Instead of wasting away, she's gained over twenty-five pounds and continues to gain weight and strength. There's no doubt in my mind that the wonder of our almighty God and His promises are involved. When we stand with Israel, He brings miracles into our lives. And we all need miracles in our lives and in our nation.

Having God's promises doesn't mean we'll never face

challenges. A few years before Tiz's recent health issue, I had a life-threatening condition myself. I'd been traveling overseas extensively and experiencing deep fatigue and severe swelling in my legs. I assumed it was from travel. One Sunday after church I couldn't get my cowboy boots on. A friend who's an RN said, "Pastor, this is not normal."

I didn't want to go, but he and Tiz got me to the ER. They did an extensive ultrasound and discovered that my lungs were full of blood clots. I also had one continuous blood clot that reached from my ankle all the way to my groin. So doctors immediately admitted me to the hospital and prepared me for surgery. I was confined to bed and not even allowed to use the restroom, because any movement could dislodge a clot. A loose clot could travel to my brain or heart and cause instant death.

After the operation the surgeon told Tiz and me that what I had was called "the widowmaker"—multiple dangerous clots that could instantly have turned my wife into a widow. He said he'd never seen such a severe case in which the patient lived to tell the story. He was a Christian and said, "God must have a very important call on your life, because He certainly saved you from death."

God is bigger than your diagnosis!

No Denial, Only Trust (Tiz)

When I was first diagnosed with ovarian cancer, I was devastated. I did not know whether I was going to live, and my life turned upside down. Thoughts hit me like a tsunami: "I have ovarian cancer. I'll have surgery in three days. I need chemo. And I still have to get a million things done."

Stacked on my desk were piles of things I had to do. Larry said, "Stop. The only thing you need to do is get with God and get yourself in a mindset to receive His miracles. Your top priority is to focus on your healing."

So every morning I took a hundred scriptures on healing and sat outside under an umbrella that Larry bought me. As I dealt with the scariest thing I had ever faced, I spoke those scriptures loudly and slowly, saturating my being with the Word of God. It took hours to read them all, and sitting still for that long is always hard for me. There are things to do, after all, and I prefer to hit the ground running. Yet I knew that this time was essential; it was the source of my future life. So by faith I did what I needed to do.

Before I say another word, I need to say this: Faith is not denying our circumstances. Faith simply denies our circumstances the right to rule and reign over us. When my diagnosis came and I heard the words "three months to live," it was surreal. I thought, "Are you kidding me?" But we hit the challenge head-on and did everything we could in every realm—the natural, spiritual, and medical. We decided to fight on every level and not allow ovarian cancer to take over our lives.

We did it all, including surgeries, chemo, and prayer. The surgeon spent eight hours removing cancer from my body. To do that, he had to remove all or part of seven organs. I won't lie. It was awful, and I have a seventeen-inch scar to prove it. The surgical recovery was hard, and from there I went straight into chemo. I felt like I'd lost my whole life, including my hair and some weight. I had to fight to live every single day.

At some point, however, the entire situation flipped, and I knew God was going to heal me. He added His *super* to our *natural*; it was a process, but I never stopped believing in healing. Because I was literally dealing with life and death, I had to transform my soul. It didn't happen in one Scripture reading or one prayer. Larry and I and our family continued to press into God's promises in faith, refusing to let fear and darkness consume us. That doesn't mean every doubt disappeared. I was still living a nightmare, but I had the assurance of what God would do. So I kept speaking it, fighting for it, and guarding my mind.

Healing from cancer, particularly this type, is not like healing from a broken limb. The threat of the disease returning hangs over you. My cancer has returned numerous times over the past six years, and I've had to do additional chemo treatments and surgeries. I'm doing chemo even now, but I've beat the odds and am doing great!

Overcoming a serious diagnosis like mine is a huge battle. You can have the victory, but it's critical to maintain a victorious, faith-filled, positive state of mind. I remember leaving the hospital after I was first diagnosed. During the car ride home, Larry, my daughters, and I all encouraged each other, saying, "It's going to be OK. God's got this. Nothing's too big for Him. He's never let us down before. His name is above all names, and He's bigger than any name or disease."

Suddenly, we all got silent, and I thought, "I know what we just said is true. But this is bigger than anything we've ever faced. We're in a whole other league now. There's got to be some kind of secret weapon of faith—some kind of atom bomb of faith to release a miracle at this level."

Then the Holy Spirit whispered and calmed my heart, "There is no new arsenal to seek. You fight this disease the same way you fought every battle from day one of your walk—by choosing to believe, trust, and obey Me."

This deeply calmed and empowered my mind and spirit. The same seed of faith that was planted nearly fifty years earlier caused us to trust God for what seemed impossible. By faith we had stepped out of the comforts of life to pioneer churches, believe God for financial provision, and do all the things God called us to do. All the challenges we faced for five decades had strengthened our faith muscles, and the weapons of warfare that would win this battle were the same weapons we always used. We had seen God bring victory in before, and we believed He would do it again. We are more than conquerors through Him who loves us (Rom. 8:37)!

Understanding this truth is one reason the journey is so important. No matter what level of difficulty you are facing, you choose to overcome by stepping into God's supernatural promises, blessings, and miracles. When you consistently do that, you activate His promises and stock your war chest—your stash of past accomplishments. When the next challenge comes (and the next and the next), you build on your stash. That is how you grow from glory to glory—from great accomplishments to even greater ones, in every area of your life.

It's Never About One Person (Tiz)

I've heard it said that a person doesn't get cancer; a family gets cancer. That is so true. Many people have been inspired by how we have handled my cancer battle. I wish I could say it was a one-and-done miracle, but it wasn't (and isn't). Our family has been standing, not only with me but also with Lion, for over six years. The fight continued through six Christmases, six Easters, six Mother's Days, six Father's Days, and all our family's birthdays, many of which were chemo treatment days. All that fighting takes a huge toll. And yet our growth as a family, spiritually and otherwise, has been profound. We are so much closer, stronger, and more determined than ever.

Every one of our kids has become a powerhouse. Our

daughter Katie is my gatekeeper and accompanies me for my medical appointments. She knows more about my situation than I do! Meanwhile, Larry has led us in faith, courage, and steadfastness. He has anchored us, calmed us, and been our rock! My daughter Anna comes along for as many appointments as she possibly can, and having her there helps us all. Larry, Anna, Brandin, the grandkids, Katie, Luke, and Jen are all powerful, positive faith warriors for Lion's and my journeys of healing. They are prayer warriors, and I'm so thankful for each of them.

Only the Lord could empower us to keep walking in victory. Only He could keep Larry preaching faith every week, regardless of our circumstances. And only He could enable me to teach and encourage others. By His grace the world gets to see us laughing, smiling, and admitting when we're frustrated, mad, or crying our eyes out. We have learned that you have to "give up to go up."[1] In order to go to new levels in faith and dominion, you have to give up and rise above certain habits, behaviors, or thought processes. We had to rise above or give up our fears, doubts, and negative thoughts and replace them with God's promises, faith, trust, and a positive outlook. We had to keep our eyes focused, not just on our problems but on His promises and destiny for us.

But this is not all about us. What God's done for us He can do for you. Our story contains living miracles because God never calls us to something without equipping us to do it. He gives us dreams that are one size too big so we can grow into them.

Larry and I never set out to be important. We set out to make an impact for God. The reason we have told so many of our stories is to draw attention not to ourselves but to God and His power. We strive to teach people to love the Lord and discover the Holy Spirit's power to transform their lives. That means learning how to win in life and overcome challenges. It means walking in God's favor, grace, and equipping strength—not denying our circumstances but facing them honestly, with God's power and promises.

No matter what you're facing—no matter how giant-sized, scary, or complicated it might seem—God is bigger. His name is above every name. And when you know and understand His names, they reveal His nature. He is

- El-HaNe'eman—The God Who Is Faithful

- El Sela—God My Rock

- El Shaddai—The All-Sufficient One

- Jehovah-Rapha—The Lord Who Heals

- Jehovah-Jireh—The Lord Who Provides

God is your refuge. He loves you and desires to move through you to change the world. If you let Him, He'll do it, even when you're in the middle of your biggest battle.

Seven years ago, when the journey through illness started for Lion and then me, our ministry took our stand with Israel and support to another level. We were doing projects over there and raising funds to help Israelis. Our friends with Keren Hayesod (United Israel Appeal) and the government agency that oversees *aliyah* (the Jewish Agency for Israel) told everybody, "If you need prayer, get Pastors Larry and Tiz to pray for you. They know how to tap into God's miracle power." One of the leaders said, "They are going through so much in their own lives, and yet they're always encouraging and praying for everyone else. Instead of focusing on their own problems, they're trying to help repair the problems of the Jewish people and nation."

Good things happen when people know you care. General Yoav Gallant, Israel's former defense minister, served directly under Bibi Netanyahu. A few years ago, when we and our kids were in Israel for the John Henry Patterson Guardian of Zion Award presentation to Larry, the government arranged for us to visit the Knesset and have a private meeting with General Gallant, who at the time was serving as the minister of Aliyah and Integration. Remember, he is among the most powerful men in the world right now, and he was willing to meet with us. So I asked, "Why would he want to meet with us?"

Our hosts said, "Because of all you do for Israel."

So we went into the Knesset, received a VIP tour of the Knesset, and went to the general's private office, where he briefed us on global affairs and issues concerning Israel. He explained how important our support and involvement with Israel was and its impact on local and global levels and expressed his appreciation. Then he took us to a special lunch that had been prepared for us.

Larry had to leave for some filming, so the kids and I stayed on and enjoyed a private luncheon with General Gallant and his leadership team. Ten or twelve of us were present, and our hosts asked, "Why are you doing all this for Israel? What is your motivation?"

I'd been having chemo treatments for several months. My hair was gone, and I wore a baseball cap, and my bald head could be seen underneath it. We shared that our passion and commitment to the nation and people of Israel was because of Genesis 12:3. Then I told them about my battle with cancer, and Luke told them about Lion and how God was healing us both.

We told them that we believed that because we were being a blessing to Israel, God was blessing us with His miracles.

As we shared this, General Gallant and his leadership team began to tear up. Imagine the weight they carried on their shoulders, yet our story touched them. They not only heard, but they also saw what we believe, and they saw God's power to heal Lion and me.

I will never forget that day or how deeply God's goodness affected them. Every time I saw General Gallant on TV, I thought of how God enabled us to tell our story to these very powerful men, essentially because we have supported and honored Israel.

We have many Jewish friends around the world. Many know Larry's testimony of how he used to be a drug addict until, suddenly, he wasn't. They have heard how God miraculously transformed Larry's soul and heart, instantly setting him free from his addiction. Larry and I are always clear about how he had to work through his anger and violence issues. But we remind them that even those bondages were broken. I also tell them how Larry asked the Lord into his heart. Most of our Jewish friends never heard anything like that before meeting us, but God placed us on a global platform, and we can share it!

Our struggles and our triumphs are never all about us. While Larry and I worked on this book, I was at City of Hope cancer treatment center for six weeks, recovering from another surgery. One day one of the oncologists who had been treating me sat on my bed and talked to me for more than an hour. My kids had sent me a photo collage of themselves, and I showed it to her. "I want you to see this," I said. "I want you to know that you're not treating one woman with cancer. This is my family. When you take care of me, this is who you're fighting for."

I also told her Lion's story, and she began to cry. (Larry shared this story with you earlier.) And she said, "Thank you for telling me that story because now I know one."

"What do you mean?" I asked.

"I have had friends whose babies have died of infant leukemia," she said. "I've studied it extensively and have never known of one child who survived the disease. Now I know one."

Without realizing it, she confirmed the great miracle that Lion had received. We'd heard such things before about the cancer Lion had. Yet this woman's reaction tore me up, because her whole life was about helping people in heartbreaking circumstances.

Our Lion (Larry)

As you know, the news of our grandson Lion's leukemia diagnosis was devastating. Lion and his parents, Luke and Jen, immediately moved into his hospital room on the children's oncology floor, where they would live for the next six months while he underwent treatment. Imagine new, adoring parents and our whole family trying to process this turn of events. All the joys of raising a newborn, playing with him, and snuggling with him were interrupted, and his medical team connected him to countless tubes, monitors, and IVs.

Lion screamed in pain as these procedures were performed. Trying to console their baby, Luke and Jen asked the doctor, "What if we decide not to do the chemo?"

He said, "Then he will die."

Through much prayer and soul-searching, we all agreed that the chemo path was right. As Tiz says so often, faith isn't the denial of what's happening; faith means facing it head-on and rising above it in every way possible, both in the natural and supernatural realms. By faith we refused to resign our-selves to the terrible reports because we know our God is a healer and miracle worker. But we faced a paradox. While we stood firmly in faith in the spiritual realm, we also had to deal with the severity of the situation in the natural realm and the responsibility to make the right choices for Lion.

Standing in faith while dealing with severe circumstances is certainly not easy; it's more like a 24/7 obstacle course. Amid a barrage of daily realities, negative reports, complications, and tough circumstances, we all made sure to keep a positive attitude, be prayerful, and stay full of faith. I told our family we were going to look for and see three positive signs each and every day. Whether big or small, we would focus on and cel-ebrate those small wins. Truly, God honored that and contin-ually brought us little miracle signs of improvement. Staying positive was by no means easy. We faced fear, sadness, and devastating reports, but we refused to allow those to dominate and define our faith or Lion's future.

Our family chose to press into prayer, praise, declaring, and envisioning God's promises coming to pass. We envisioned the day we would celebrating Lion's release from the hospital and being declared cancer free. We imagined the day when we could take him outside the hospital walls and play on swing sets and roll around in the grass. We dealt with the problems as they were presented. But we chose not to focus on those problems but on God's promises.

We didn't see a giant, one-and-done miracle healing for Lion, but we saw thousands of smaller miracles that added up to his giant miracle. This is where we coined the phrase "mir-acles by the moment." God truly is bigger than our diagnosis!

Amid all the difficult reports, some very positive news came for Lion. Doctors ordered a test to see whether he had a negative gene that would lower his chances of survival. When the test showed he did not have that gene, his chances of survival increased greatly. Then another test showed that Lion had a positive gene that would help him fight cancer. So once again, his chances of survival greatly improved. Miraculously, this gene, which develops only in the teen years, was found in baby Lion. We called it the God gene!

That first day began six months of daily, intensive chemotherapy. Lion also received twelve other medicines through his IV each day. They were added to help protect his heart, lungs, and other organs from the very strong chemo—so strong that it caused Lion's tiny hands and feet to peel.

Fifty days after Lion's chemo began, a bone marrow test showed that his blood was cancer free! But with children's cancer, if you start a plan, you must finish it. If you quit midway, the disease can rebound. In fact, Lion would be on chemo for three years, with all of us standing on the promises of God for his healing and cure.

The day Lion was released from the hospital, the nurses and doctors had a party for him and his parents. The whole medical team cried tears of joy saying, "We needed to see a victory." For these professionals who were surrounded by sadness and very sick children, as well as for other struggling families, Lion's story and our family's contagious faith and optimism were a light.

As we've mentioned, Lion is now seven years old and cancer free. He's doing incredibly well and has defied the odds! He is amazing, brilliant, full of joy, strong, healthy, and growing fast. His first-grade classmates voted him the kindest kid in class because he's always happy and encouraging others. He's also our miracle boy and a living testimony of God's love. From day one, our family stood in faith, on God's promises of life. We declared that Lion would live, thrive, and not die.

We did everything we could in the natural realm to benefit his health. We decided to go forward with the chemo, but we believed God to do what seemed impossible.

Giving Joy

When you're in the midst of trauma or trials, your human nature can turn inward and preoccupy you with self-concern, mounting needs, and self-preservation. When our family faced devastating times, we ramped up our works for God and His people and looked for ways to bless, encourage, and be a light to others. We were called to *tikkun olam*—to repair the broken world even when ours was broken.

Words of encouragement are vital, but we're also called to act. Luke and Jen started a nonprofit called Free Music. Music is a major part of Lion's life. He has perfect pitch and a photographic memory and has been reading since he was two years old. He plays the drums, piano, and guitar and is composing his own music and songs. So Luke and Jen gather donated musical instruments and give them free of charge to kids who are battling cancer. The instruments help the kids focus on fun by making music and get their minds off their disease.

We've learned that the greatest way to gain joy is to give joy. Providing instruments to sick children gives them and their families hope, love, and joy. It shows them they are not forgotten, and one little girl has already recorded her own album!

With God, the impossible is made possible. Only the Lord could have done the miracles that Lion, Tiz, and I have experienced. We are 1,000 percent convinced that the source of the miracles we have shared is threefold:

1. God almighty—His love, covenant promises, and supernatural miracle power

2. Jesus Christ our Savior—lived, died, and was resurrected to give us life abundant

3. Genesis 12:3—God's covenant promise that as we bless Israel, He will bless us

Yes! God is bigger than your diagnosis—*way* bigger.

Chapter 16

FROM JUNKIE ALL THE WAY TO JERUSALEM

FIFTY YEARS AGO I could not have known what was on the other side of my yes to God. He led me step by step as I trusted Him for the next one. Now I can look back and say, "Look at what the Lord has done. Look how far He's taken me."

I was an angry, violent, drugged-up hippie. People said, "Once a junkie, always a junkie," but God had other plans. He didn't look at the outside of me. He looked at the inside. All He needed was a vessel who was willing to have relationship with Him. He needed someone who would allow Him to flow through them. I can tell you that if you let Him have that control, He will take you on your own journey of destiny.

"For I know the thoughts that I think toward you, says the LORD, thoughts of peace and not of evil, to give you a future and a hope" (Jer. 29:11). This scripture has proven true in my life. The Lord even brought my soulmate at just the right time. He knew that Tiz was exactly what I needed and that I was exactly what she needed. We weren't duplicates, because that wouldn't have worked. We came from completely different backgrounds, and God brought us together on a collision course of destiny. We said yes to an unknown future with Him, let go of the past, and stepped out in faith. Our unique gifts and strengths made us stronger as a team, and we became a single force for the kingdom of God.

Please know that I'm doing what King David and the apostle Paul did: I'm boasting about the Lord and what He's done. I know where I came from and what He delivered me from. I also know what He is willing to do in you, whatever your circumstances.

On my journey from junkie to Jerusalem, I've been challenged by others' faith and accomplishments and the directions they've taken. So often, the guidance of the Holy Spirit made little natural sense to me. Yet through faith, hard work, dedication, and trusting God, Tiz and I have never seen our dreams fall short. When the path we were on was challenged or needed to be redirected, we clung to and trusted God's promise in Romans 8:28 and kept pressing on, never allowing ourselves to be disillusioned.

The real story is that God has always shown Himself strong on our behalf and made a way, even when there seemed to be none. And He will do the same for you. Dream big, because your God is big. Refuse to be limited by the natural circumstances of your life. Choose to trust God, and He will break you out of them. Let Him add His super to your natural. What might seem impossible becomes possible with Him. Tiz and I have learned that with God, life makes sense. Therefore, we were happy when we had nothing, and we are equally happy with much more. Our happiness has never depended on stuff; it has come from enjoying the journey as His presence goes with us.

Moses told the Lord, "If your Presence does not go with us, do not bring us up from here" (Exod. 33:15). God has sent

Tiz, me, and our kids into some hard places, but we always knew His presence was with us. Hard did not mean bad. Even through the most difficult times, we enjoyed the journey, because His peace was on us and the Holy Spirit empowered us. (See Philippians 4:7; 1 Corinthians 12:11.)

It's so exciting to see your life evolve as God meets you where you are and blesses you. It's even more exciting when God uses your life to *tikkun olam*—to make the world a better place by helping to repair the broken places for others.

In ancient Hebrew there is no word for *coincidence*. The fact that you are reading this book is not happenstance. God led you to hear our story so it might influence your future. May God give you hope, inspiration, and grace as He equips you to lay hold of and accomplish His great vision, plan, and destiny for your life. I urge you to pray that God would bless you so you can be a blessing. Then, when you're faithful with little, He will trust you with much (Luke 16:10), and your "much" will increase.

Our story demonstrates two basic points: (1) that God can take the most messed up human beings and transform them into new creations and (2) that He wants to use them to be light, to bridge gaps, to break down walls, and to impact the world for Him. He wants to take every human being on a junkie-to-Jerusalem journey of destiny.

To Jerusalem

When it comes to Israel and the ways in which God has used us on Israel's behalf, Tiz and I were reluctant to share at first. Now we are compelled to do so. People often equate humility with not mentioning what God does through them. They believe it's prideful to talk about it, but that idea is not biblical. David wrote, "My mouth will tell of your righteous acts, of your deeds of salvation all the day, for their number is past my knowledge. With the mighty deeds of the Lord GOD I will come; I will remind them of your righteousness, yours alone" (Ps. 71:15–16, ESV).

We are doing what David described: We're shouting from the housetops about what He's done, giving Him the glory and not ourselves. Sometimes pride keeps our mouths shut. So we will boast in the Lord. Personally, I did not ask for or pursue the Derek Prince encounter. And none of what our family has done with Israel was for notoriety's sake. We did it because it was what God directed us to do—and it needed to be done. The important Israel piece of our story connects the miracles that God has done in and through our lives. We are testifying to what He can do through any willing vessel.

Little did I know that on that day in Capernaum thirty-plus years ago, we stepped into the most important phase of our destiny. The trail of events since then has astounded us! Bible prophecy unfolds daily, right before our eyes. Think about it: When God inspired the ancient end-time prophecies, He saw the days that you and I are living in, and He saw us taking up the mantles to be part of our times!

Yes, *From Junkie to Jerusalem* is the testimony of our lives. But it is also about God's call on your life. It is about your part in what God is doing in the world and in Israel. So get ready and get excited, because as you hear about our journey, you'll be inspired about your journey with God!

Contrary to what some people believe, the Jewish roots teaching and our embrace of Israel do not detract from the New Testament or the new covenant in Christ. They clarify and fulfill it! Jesus said, "Do not think that I have come to abolish the Law or the Prophets. I have not come to abolish, but to fulfill" (Matt. 5:17, MEV). Jesus didn't come to start a new religion.

He came to bring us back to God and reveal the truth in His Word. When we grasp the mysteries revealed in the Hebrew, we become open to the blessings that bring hope, change, miracles, and the knowledge that nothing is impossible with God.

It's time to take the limits off yourself and off God. Get a God-sized vision for your life, your future, your finances, and your family. Let God be God. There are no boundaries on what He can do—in you, for you, or through you. Let Him lead you, equip you, and strengthen you with His favor, grace, and power. You might struggle with low self-esteem or self-worth. Even as believers we tend to struggle with these issues. We ask ourselves, "Who am I to be used by God?"

Here's the thing: Every great Bible leader asked that question. David was the runt of the litter, yet God used him to change the world. Rahab was a down-and-out harlot, but God used her to accomplish His plans. Peter was a crude, rough fisherman who denied the Lord, yet God used him in building the church.

Never let your past determine your future. When you allow God almighty to take up residence in your heart, mind, soul, and body, His DNA becomes your DNA. Let Him give you dreams that are one size too big. Then let Him grow you into them. After all, if you can do it on your own, you're not dreaming big enough.

Biblical Citizenship

For many years, but especially the past few years, I've realized how imperative it is for God's people to engage in the political choices and policies that deeply affect our values, lifestyles, and future. That's why I teach on this subject. Because Tiz and I have lived outside America and traveled the world, we have seen the far-reaching consequences in and through nations that aren't built on biblical values. We Americans take a lot for granted, including our rights to freedom of speech and religion, as well as the right to choose our moral values, way of life, and prosperity.

On Wednesday nights at church, we have a service called Biblical Citizenship. We teach about our biblical responsibility to be aware of the facts and live in ways that impact the world with biblical values. We invite guest speakers from political, educational, law enforcement, medical, and business realms to provide insight into the policies that affect us. We encourage our people to get involved in issues and leadership at a grass-roots level and thereby influence the direction of their families, schools, cities, and nations.

So many of God's people have a wrong idea about politics and religion needing to be separated. Many don't vote or really care about what goes on in political realms. This has never been God's plan. As His light and His people we are meant to drive back the darkness and establish His dominion in every area of life. How can we do that if we don't involve ourselves in making decisions that impact policies and create the future of our nations?

Especially in the current age, liberal agendas have changed our nation's trajectory. These agendas direct political realms, political candidates, and choices that deeply infringe on our rights, lifestyles, and freedom to raise our children and run our businesses. These agendas even affect our churches. They stunt our freedom of speech and thought.

I believe that as God's children, we must take a stand, use our voice, cultivate influence, and establish God's dominion, nationally and locally, in our schools and in our families. I've heard Christians say, "It's all in God's hands." Really? When has that ever been the case? God says throughout the Bible that He moves through His people, not through lightning bolts from heaven.

We all know the scripture "If My people who are called by My name will humble themselves, and pray and seek My face, and turn from their wicked ways, then I will hear from heaven, and will forgive their sin and heal their land" (2 Chron. 7:14). In other words, *if* we (do this), *then* He (does that). God has always raised up leaders who will fight the darkness and redirect the courses the enemy tries to establish. Too many of God's people sit on the sidelines—apathetic, ignorant, intimidated, or silent. That's why we encourage our people to know the issues, examine the candidates, find out what's going on in our schools, get involved, and be part of *tikkun olam*, repairing the broken world.

Recently, a candidate who was tearing down conservatives shouted, "Mind your own [expletive] business!"

To that we shout back, "Mind *your* own business!"

Liberals have pushed their morals, lifestyles, and agendas on our schools, families, and churches. They're diminishing parental rights and exposing our children to ungodly lifestyles. They're normalizing those lifestyles and desensitizing children to ungodly morals and values. With the darkness pressing against the doors of our churches, we have no choice but to push back. If we as God's people don't stand up, who will? And if we don't, then what?

Unbiblical agendas are trying to dim or extinguish not only our light but the light and presence of God Himself.

Unite the Light

At New Beginnings, we created a rally called Unite the Light. We say, "If we are the light of the world, why don't we unite the light?" So we invite Hispanic, white, and black pastors to bring their worship teams and congregations to the rally and let our unity and light shine brightly to the city and the world.

The idea is to create a multiplying impact. One candle here and one candle over there will give some light. But if you put all the candles together, get along with one another, and unite the light, the darkness cannot survive. Darkness flourishes in the absence of light. By uniting the light, we can push out the darkness.

Evil is encroaching and trying to take over. Unfortunately, believers and religious groups are so fragmented over doctrine and other issues that our light to the world is dimmed. If we would lay down our differences, join together, and unite the light, we could be an incredibly powerful force for good and for God in the world.

Tiz and I are very vocal in this, but a lot of pastors are silent because of the so-called separation of church and state and the fear of losing their 501(c)(3) status. The separation of church and state was never meant to keep the church out of politics and government. It was meant to keep the state or government out of church business. Our nation was founded on the right of churches to be ruled not by the government but by God.

Kelly Shackelford is the president and CEO of First Liberty Institute and "a constitutional scholar who has argued before the United States Supreme Court, testified before the U.S. House and Senate and has won numerous landmark First Amendment and religious liberty cases, including three land-mark religious liberty victories in the U.S. Supreme Court."[1] When I was at a meeting with President Trump, I asked Mr. Shackelford about church-state issues, and he said, "Being a pastor doesn't mean you forfeit your freedom of speech. As a pastor you can say whatever you want. Now, you cannot tell people, 'You can't work for me unless you vote a certain way,' or 'You can't be in my business if you don't vote that way.'"

From the pulpit or among staff or potential staff members, I can't tell people how to vote, but I can tell them my opinions and what the Bible says about issues. And I can tell them how I will vote. Recent polls show that 80 percent of Evangelicals want their pastors to address current issues in the world and politics.[2] As a pastor I'm allowed to speak about the issues because freedom of speech is my constitutional right.

When Peter and John were arrested by religious leaders, those who saw the disciples' "boldness...marveled" and "realized that they had been with Jesus" (Acts 4:13). That boldness was part of the disciples' walk with Jesus. So Tiz and I don't hold anything back. We can't be bought. And we will stand up for what the Word of God says, whether it's politically correct or not.

Some Christians misunderstand Isaiah 9:6, which says of the Messiah, "The government will be upon His shoulder." They take the statement to mean that God takes care of everything and believers should not be involved with shaping government. The true meaning is that the government (consisting of God-led, Spirit-filled men and women) should be established and stand upon His shoulder, meaning God's principles and foundations, His Word, and His commandments.

God never called His people to cower or let evil run rampant. He has always called us to ride out the storm and fight for His dominion to be established and drive back the evil forces. That sounds stark, because the darkness is real. But understand this: We don't hate anybody. I won't forget that Jesus loved me and rescued me where I was and as I was. That's biblical.

How Would Jesus Vote?

Elections are not popularity or personality contests. They are the choices we make for the direction and values we want for ourselves and for our families, nation, and future. A recent poll showed that around 32 million Christian churchgoers were unlikely to vote in the 2024 US election.[3] As an American citizen, a Christian, and a pastor, I find that statistic shocking. Each of us has an obligation to be part of our nation's direction and destiny. It saddens me (and yes, it makes me mad) to think of all it took to build this great nation—not only through prayer, hope, and ideology but also through hard labor, dedication, and sacrifice. It is mind-boggling to think of how easily it is being dismantled and upended by belief systems, values, and morals that are opposite to those of our founding ideals.

By not voting or being involved in politics, Christians are turning our nation over to ungodly values and ideologies. Burying our heads in the sand will not save us from this fate. The choices, decisions, and policies that result will affect every one of us, as well as the generations after us.

Hebrews 11 tells us about the heroes of our faith and their accomplishments. Scripture also points out their flaws and shortcomings. God's biblical heroes were not perfect people. They were humans like us who yielded their lives to God and His purposes. Today's world leaders and politicians are not perfect people. Neither are you and I. If God waited for the perfect man or woman to use in this world, nothing would ever happen. God has always looked for people He could use despite their shortcomings. He has sought people who aligned themselves with His values and stood up to make a difference. He is still looking for those people.

Jesus said that we believers are "the salt of the earth" (Matt. 5:13). Salt is used to keep food from rotting. It is an invaluable preservative with a distinct purpose. Jesus calls you and me to be the salt of the earth. Our purpose as Christians, believers, or Jews is to keep our nations and the world from rotting away. Jesus warned that "if the salt loses its flavor...it is then good for nothing but to be thrown out and trampled underfoot by men" (v. 13). If you aren't the salt that has kept its flavor, you're good for nothing. You're going to be thrown out and trampled on, and the world is going to walk all over you.

Think about when Mordecai told Esther that she needed to go before the king "for such a time as this" (Est. 4:14). She feared for her life and rightly so. Mordecai essentially said, "Don't think that you and your family will escape Haman's treachery. You need to stand up, and if you don't, God will raise up somebody else."

The same is true today. We can refuse to make a stand. We can try our best to blend in with the world and not make waves. But we will not escape the effects of evil and sin in the world. Believe me, I understand. As a pastor, taking a stand on moral, worldly, political, or controversial issues is difficult. You can't please everybody, and you will lose some people who don't want to hear what you say. We decided a long time ago that we would "choose who we lose." One thing I'm sure of is that we are on the right side of God, and that's what matters.

We must be aware of what's happening all around us. We all know the saying "The only thing necessary for evil to rule is for good people to do nothing." Let me challenge you, as we challenge ourselves every day: Ask the Lord what He's doing in the world and how you can be part of it. Ask what your role is as a light and an influence. Let the light shine in your home and family. Carry it to the schools, communities, cities, nations, and even the world. Be bold, stand up, and speak up—always standing with God on the issues that concern Him and us as His people. Let Him fill your heart with wisdom, direction, confidence, and anointing to stand for truth. Live the truth and walk it out. Make a difference in the world. And remember *tikkun olam*: Repair the broken world and broken people.

Our Unite the Light theme has played into our journey

to Jerusalem. Our connections with Israel have evolved from projects of charity into friendships and alliances in the political realms with Jewish leaders in Israel and the world. Remember that all nations are formed and evolve from political ideologies and belief systems. Christianity and Judaism are tied together and are meant to be united in their biblical influence and their calls to bring God's light and dominion to the world. When people ask, "What business does the church or religion have in politics?" my answer is "All kinds of business." Evil forces have brought evil to our doorsteps. It is our duty and obligation to drive back those forces and establish God's dominion and authority in all the earth.

Politically, as a nation, we should stand with Israel. The blessing of Genesis 12:3 applies not only to individuals but also to nations. One of the major reasons the United States has been so blessed is because we have stood with Israel and the Jewish people. The protection around Israel extends around us. Our leaders might think we are protecting Israel, but the truth is, they are protecting us. God's favor on them comes to us.

David Friedman served as the United States ambassador to Israel from 2017 to 2021. He also served as an adviser to Donald Trump during his first successful presidential campaign. Ambassador Friedman told me that he listens intently when I speak. It now seems fitting to share a statement from his talk at a recent Israel Allies Foundation (IAF) event.

> In 1941, there were 18 million Jews in the world. Today, there are only about 15 million in the world, including about 7 million living in Israel. Israel is a small nation. We are small and we need friends. To have someone like Pastor Larry Huch and others who have this huge reach to millions of people preaching to love Israel is huge to

us. I don't think you understand what it means to the Jewish people. We're so used to being persecuted, driven out of our homes and lands, destroyed or slaughtered, and on the short end of history, basically for our entire existence. And in that entire period, we looked far and wide, and we'd say in the Psalms, "I lift my eyes up unto the heavens. Where's my salvation coming from?" Well, of course there is God, but that was it. It was just God. God has kept us around. Now we have something else, something we never had before. We have this incredible bond to this beautiful, wonderful Christian community that we just haven't had before. It's changed everything. It's just changed absolutely everything. And it enables me to go and speak to the president of the United States and say, "Mr. President, this is what we ought to do because it's the right thing to do and because a hundred million people want you to do it as well, okay?" That was never a conversation anybody could have had on the Jewish issue up until the last decade. So the gratitude and appreciation we as Jews have is enormous.

Why are we fighting to be Jewish or to support the Jewish people? Why is it worth the effort? It's so difficult to do. Why should we do this? And the answer is because it's all about this magnificent 3,500-year legacy that was given to the Jewish people that we're so blessed to continue. We are standing on the shoulders of heroes, of prophets, of kings, for 3,500 years. I'm not breaking that chain; none of us want to break that chain. It is that we are the transmitter of the wellspring of the values that have made America a great nation. Make Israel a great nation. Make Christianity a great faith. Make Judaism a great faith. It's all on our shoulders. We can't give it up. October 7th was the worst day of my life, other than the day I lost my father and my mother. Since October 7th, we know who our friends are.

> We knew who our enemies are. We know what our challenges are, and now we have the ability without hesitation, without doubt, to rise up and meet our challenges and to really, really change the course of history. And in doing so, to fulfill the will of God. I hope you'll all join me on this effort, on this mission. Thank you so much for all you and your people are doing for Israel.[4]

At the same event Josh Reinstein, president of the IAF, reiterated the importance of Christian support for Israel. "When Christians stand with Israel and the Jewish people, it's not merely an act of faith; it's a profound commitment to justice and our shared Judeo-Christian values," he said. "Faith-based diplomacy is responsible for around 80 percent of Israel's diplomatic successes today."[5]

Each year, the IAF publishes a list of Israel's top fifty Christian allies, and for the third year in a row, I had the great honor of being listed in the top three. The IAF stated that "the Christian leaders included in this exclusive list express their love and support for the State of Israel through meaningful action, rooted in their deeply held faith," noting that everyone chosen in 2024 had continued to advocate for Israel after the October 7 Hamas attack.

How blessed we are to be laboring with such people as David Friedman, Josh Reinstein, Sam Grundwerg of Keren Heyasod, and all the others we have or have not mentioned. Recently, during a live stream at our church, Sam Grundwerg updated us on the impact of our projects in Israel after the October 7 massacre:

> Pastors Larry and Tiz Huch are some of the greatest friends Israel has in the world today. They are tireless in their efforts of standing, supporting, donating,

advocating for the nation of Israel. Their strong, courageous, bold voices and their charitable projects have changed...the lives of hundreds of thousands of people in Israel and around the world.

Pastor Larry was one of the first people to come to Israel and visit the actual sites of the October 7 terrorist massacres. Together we witnessed, filmed, and documented these barbaric atrocities. Pastor, Tiz, and their family have relentlessly spoken of and shown the footage as a witness of truth to the world of the atrocities committed against Israel. They have encouraged and shown the nation and people of Israel, and Jews around the world, that they are not alone and vow with them, "Never again!"

We are so thankful for Pastors Larry and Tiz and their family, the staff and people of New Beginnings Church, and Larry Huch Ministries, who have been an answer to the prayers of so many in Israel. You all truly demonstrate *tikkun olam*—helping to repair a broken world. May the Huchs' hearts, vision, and actions be infectious to all that know them and hear their message.

From Israel to all of you, thank you and God bless you!

And we thank God for all of them!

I'm always hesitant to speak about my accomplishments. Tiz and I talk about these things not to bring attention to ourselves but to bring attention to God, His promises, and His power to use the least of us to make a difference for Him. None of us knows what's on the other side of our yes to God.

Over the last several years, I have had the humbling honor of speaking to Christian and Jewish leaders all over the world to raise awareness and support for Israel. This is the primary focus of our global TV program and media ministries. The response has been incredible, and we are so grateful for this great privilege. The Lord has continually opened new opportunities for us to be a voice for Israel and the Jewish people. Our message about the Jewish roots of Christianity has been tearing down walls that have divided Christians and Jews for thousands of years. And our work with Keren Heyasod and the IAF has allowed us to influence leaders and governments to stand with Israel.

Amazingly, I've also had the privilege of working with many of the top leaders in the United States, Israel, Brazil, and other nations. And Tiz and I have been able to help influence our own US government by encouraging Christians to vote for biblical values. It's astonishing to think about all the things Tiz and I have been able to do in our lives.

Whenever I speak about supporting Israel, I end by telling the stories of Lion's and Tiz's miraculous healings. We know without a doubt that Tiz and Lion are both alive and thriving today because our family has lived according to Genesis 12:3. God has blessed us as we have blessed Israel.

Remember the phone call I received when I was in Israel saying the lion would roar? That scripture (Joel 3:16) certainly has broad significance, but in light of our family's situation, I can honestly say that the testimony of our little Lion's miracle truly is roaring from Jerusalem.

If God can take a junkie from the streets of St. Louis and use him to reach people on the streets and in the government of Israel, imagine what He can do in, for, and through you.

As Long as You Have Breath

As our journey through these pages ends, I pray my story has shown you that God knows everything about you and has a plan and purpose for your life. Your move is simply to open yourself to Him and let Him guide you. It doesn't matter what your circumstances are. Your age doesn't matter either. As long as you have breath, the Lord wants you. You might be a junkie who can't string two sentences together, like I was. Yet the Lord wants you and has a plan for your future.

Maybe you know the Lord and are serving Him. Or maybe you have fallen away—a little or a lot. Maybe your life with Him is limited or feeling stagnant, but you want to come back to the Lord, move into a deeper relationship with Him, and press into all that He has for you. Or maybe you've never given your life to the Lord but now want to. Whatever your story, please pray this prayer with me, from your heart:

> *Father, I come to You right now in the name of Jesus. I know I've sinned. We've all sinned. But I know this: You love me so much that You sent Jesus Christ, Your Son, to pay in full the price for all my sins. I receive Jesus as my Lord and Savior. Lord, come into my heart. Make me a new person. Give me a new heart and a new life. Use my life to make an impact on this world, and help me to be all that You have called me to be. I step out of the limitations of this world and step into Your never-ending love, promises, blessings, and miracles. I cast off every limitation, bondage, and hindrance to my life, family, finances, and future, declaring that every curse is broken and reversed, and every blessing is released—not someday but today.*
>
> *I know You are a great God who has a great future for me. Take me from being a victim to being a victor. Equip me to overcome every*

obstacle in my path. I am more than a conqueror through You who loves me. Put me on a journey of destiny. Nothing is impossible for You, so I take the limits off my life, family, and future, and I receive You. Lord, give me a heart after Your own heart so I can know You, love You, serve You, love people, love Your Word, make a stand for You in the world, and love and stand with Israel. Bless me greatly, Lord, so that I can be a great blessing to others. Thank You, Lord! Amen.

Tiz and I are so thankful for all God has done in our lives and for all the people He has brought in to be a part of this journey—including you. What an honor and privilege it is to be part of what God is doing in the world and through His people. And you and I get to be part of it!

Yes, our journey has been incredible so far, but we're just getting started! God bless you greatly so you can bless others. Our world needs you!

Me in 1953 with my older brother in front of our flat in St. Louis, Missouri, and in high school in 1966 (right)

Before and after: Me in college in 1970 before I came to faith (left) and in Flagstaff, Arizona, in 1975 after I gave my life to the Lord (right)

Tiz and me in Flagstaff, Arizona, in 1976

On an outreach in Sedona, Arizona, sharing my testimony in 1976

Tiz and I had no idea what God had in store for us when we got married February 12, 1977, in Helena, Montana. It has been an amazing adventure.

Henry's Market and Liquors became the site of our first church building in Santa Fe, New Mexico. We later refurbished an old bar to serve as our church building as the congregation grew.

In 1979, teaching at an outdoor service in Santa Fe, New Mexico

God moved mightily at our church in Adelaide, South Australia, where we ministered to over forty nationalities.

In Adelaide, Tiz and I had the honor of knowing Aunty Betty (far left), an amazing aboriginal woman who became a surrogate grandma to our kids.

ABOVE: We continued to see lives touched when we began pastoring in Melbourne, Australia. RIGHT: In 1987 at our church in Melbourne with Tiz, Luke, Anna, and baby Katie, who was born in Melbourne

LEFT: Tiz and me in 2003 at a pastors conference at New Beginnings in Portland, Oregon. BELOW: Shortly after we launched New Beginnings in Dallas, I rode my motorcycle on the platform for a sermon called "Jesus, the Friend to Sinners."

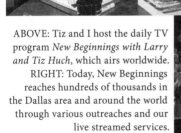

ABOVE: Tiz and I host the daily TV program *New Beginnings with Larry and Tiz Huch*, which airs worldwide. RIGHT: Today, New Beginnings reaches hundreds of thousands in the Dallas area and around the world through various outreaches and our live streamed services.

I toured sites devastated by the horrific terrorist attack on October 7, 2023, with Shmulik Fried (above) of Friends of Israel and Sam Grundwerg (right), world chairman of Keren Hayesod (United Israel Appeal). While touring, I met Israel's new defense minister, Israel Katz (below).

My daughter Katie and I took this photo with Rachel Goldberg-Polin, mother of Hersh Goldberg-Polin, who was kidnapped and murdered by Hamas after the October 7 attack. Katie and I met with Rachel and heard her heartbreaking story during a visit in March 2024.

New Beginnings and Larry Huch Ministries have donated sixteen ambulances to Israel, including three military-grade ambulances. On average, each ambulance saves roughly 10,000 lives. Tiz and I (above) have been able to go to Israel to dedicate most of these ambulances. In 2024, Katie went with me to dedicate a bomb shelter (right), one of thirty we have donated, and one of the three military-grade ambulances (below).

Our ministry has had the honor of providing food, supplies, love, support, and other assistance to Holocaust survivors in Israel.

We also have helped tens of thousands of Jewish people, like this family from Ethiopia, make *aliyah* to Israel.

In 2024, I had the honor of speaking at galas in Bangkok, Hong Kong, and Singapore sponsored by Friends of Israel at Keren Hayesod, where I talked about the importance of supporting Israel and the Jewish people's right to exist and live in the land.

Rabbi Daniel Lapin, whom I consider a great friend, spoke at New Beginnings in October 2024.

Knesset Christian Allies Caucus is at **Waldorf Astoria Jerusalem.**
February 3 at 4:35 AM · Jerusalem, Israel · 🌐

I was incredibly humbled to receive the John Patterson Award from the Israeli government in 2024. Here, Tiz and I are pictured with several Israeli dignitaries: Sam Grundwerg, world chairman of Keren Hayesod, is to my right, and former Israeli Minister of Defense Maj. Gen. Yoav Gallant is standing next to him; Josh Reinstein, director of the Knesset Christian Allies Caucus, is standing to the left of Tiz.

God has opened some incredible doors for me to share the need to support Israel, including connecting me with former Brazilian President Jair Bolsonaro. In 2022, he and I participated in the March for Jesus in Brazil (left), led by my friends Apostle Estevam and Bishop Sonia Hernandes (below), founders of Reborn in Christ Church.

Former US Ambassador to Israel David M. Friedman and me at the 2023 March of the Living in Poland

Here I am posing at an Israel Allies Foundation event in 2023 with Governor Mike Huckabee, who was appointed US ambassador to Israel after President Trump's reelection.

Sam Grundwerg, world chairman of Keren Hayesod, and Ron Dermer, former Israeli ambassador to the United States and later Israel's minister of strategic affairs, joined me in teaching at a service at New Beginnings.

After a Standing With Israel event at our church, I had the pleasure of taking Ron Dermer (right) to a Dallas Cowboys game. It was at that game that Ron, out of nowhere, put me on the phone with Prime Minister Netanyahu.

One of the most exciting moments for me and the nation of Israel was when the US embassy was moved to Jerusalem in 2017. I was there to mark the occasion with Prime Minister Benjamin Netanyahu and his wife, Sara, and President Donald Trump and his wife, Melania.

Rabbi Israel Meir Lau, former Chief Rabbi of Israel, with me at the March of the Living event in Poland in 2024

Me with Prime Minister Benjamin Netanyahu at a gala in 2020

Israeli President Isaac Herzog and wife, Michal, with me, Tiz, and Katie at their residence in Jerusalem in January 2022

US Senator Ted Cruz and me at an event supporting Israel in 2024

Texas Governor Greg Abbott with Tiz and Katie at an event in Houston in 2017 aimed at supporting Israel and the Jewish people

I have had the great pleasure of getting to know Samarian Governor Yossi Dagan, whom I visited in June 2024.

225

Tiz and I know that by blessing Israel, the Lord has blessed us and our family. Shown from left are our grandson Judah, son-in-law Brandin, daughter Anna, granddaughter Aviva Shalom, me, grandson Lion (sitting between me and Tiz), daughter Katie, daughter-in-law Jen, son Luke, and grandson Asher.

My mom and me when she visited Dallas in 2015 (left) and Tiz and me in 2024 (right)

NOTES

Chapter 1

1. "The Seven Places Jesus Shed His Blood," Larry Huch Ministries, March 28, 2024, https://larryhuchministries.com/blog/seven-places/.

Chapter 2

1. Bernie Taupin and Elton John, "Tiny Dancer," Universal Music Publishing Group, 1971.

Chapter 3

1. Jason Socrates Bardi, "Serotonin Receptors and Drug Abuse," Scripps Research Institute, accessed November 12, 2024, https://www.scripps.edu/newsandviews/e_20030929/parsons.html; "Cocaine," National Institute on Drug Abuse, accessed November 12, 2024, https://nida.nih.gov/research-topics/cocaine#work.
2. Amy Tikkanen, "Pablo Escobar: Eight Interesting Facts About the King of Cocaine," *Britannica*, accessed November 12, 2024, https://www.britannica.com/list/pablo-escobar-8-interesting-facts-about-the-king-of-cocaine.
3. *American Made*, directed by Doug Liman, Universal Pictures, 2017; *Escobar: Paradise Lost*, directed by Andrea Di Stefano, Radius TWC, 2015; *Blow*, directed by Ted Demme, New Line Cinema, 2001; *Narcos*, created by Carlo Bernard, Chris Brancato, and Doug Miro, Netflix, 2015–2017.

Chapter 5

1. John G. Niehardt, *Black Elk Speaks: Being the Life Story of a Holy Man of the Oglala Sioux* (Lincoln, NE: University of Nebraska Press, 1988).

Chapter 6

1. *The Gospel Road: A Story of Jesus*, directed by Robert Elfstrom, 20th Century Fox, 1973; "Soundtracks," *The Gospel Road: A Story of Jesus*, IMDb.com, accessed November 14, 2024, https://www.imdb.com/title/tt0070125/soundtrack/.
2. "The Alternative Jesus: Psychedelic Christ," *Time*, June 21, 1971, https://time.com/archive/6839039/the-alternative-jesus-psychedelic-christ/; "Religion: Many Things to Many Men," *Time*, June 21, 1971, https://time.com/archive/6839040/religion-many-things-to-many-men/; "The Great Jesus Rally in Dallas," *Time*, June 30, 1972.

Chapter 8

1. Beth Shelburne, "Angola's Angst: A Disquieting Tour Through the Largest Maximum Security Prison in the Nation," *The Bitter Southerner*, January 21, 2020, https://bittersoutherner.com/angolas-angst-louisiana-penitentiary.
2. The Doobie Brothers, vocalists, "Jesus Is Just Alright," by Arthur Reynolds, *Toulouse Street*, Warner Bros., 1972; "Jesus Is Just Alright," Songfacts, accessed November 15, 2024, https://www.songfacts.com/facts/the-doobie-brothers/jesus-is-just-alright.

Chapter 9

1. Peggy Lee, vocalist, "Is That All There Is?," by Jerry Leiber and Mike Stoller, *Is That All There Is?*, Capitol Records, 1969.
2. C. S. Lewis, *Mere Christianity* (New York: HarperOne, 1980), 136–37.

Chapter 11

1. "What Does 'Bashert' Mean?," My Jewish Learning, accessed November 15, 2024, https://www.myjewishlearning.com/article/what-does-bashert-mean.
2. David Wilkerson, *The Cross and the Switchblade*, with John and Elizabeth Sherrill (New York: Bernard Geis Associates, 1963).
3. *The Cross and the Switchblade*, directed by Don Murray, Gateway Films, 1970.
4. Corrie ten Boom, *The Hiding Place*, 35th anniversary ed., with Elizabeth and John Sherrill (Grand Rapids, MI: Chosen Books, 2006), 227.

Chapter 12

1. "Ghettos," Holocaust Encyclopedia, last edited December 4, 2019, https://encyclopedia.ushmm.org/content/en/article/ghettos.
2. Merriam-Webster.com, s.v. "ghetto," accessed November 20, 2024, https://www.merriam-webster.com/dictionary/ghetto.
3. Merriam-Webster.com, s.v. "ghetto."
4. "Ghetto and Gutter," Thesaurus.Plus, accessed October 25, 2024, https://thesaurus.plus/related/ghetto/gutter.
5. Katarzyna Prochwicz and Artur Sobczyk, "Syndrom jerozolimski. Objawy, przebieg i kontekst kulturowy [Jerusalem Syndrome: Symptoms, Course and Cultural Context]," *Psychiatria polska* 45, no. 2 (2011): 289–96, https://pubmed.ncbi.nlm.nih.gov/21714216/.

Chapter 13

1. The term literally means "repair of the world." "Tikkun Olam," ShirAmi, accessed November 18, 2024, https://www.shirami.org/tikkunolam.html.

Chapter 14

1. "Tikkun Olam," Shir Ami, accessed November 18, 2024, https://www.shirami.org/tikkunolam.html.
2. Yanki Tauber, comp., "Charity: An Anthology," Chabad.org, accessed November 18, 2024, https://www.chabad.org/library/article_cdo/aid/3056/jewish/Charity-an-Anthology.htm.
3. Yossi Lew, "What Is 'Aliyah'?," Chabad.org, accessed November 18, 2024, https://www.chabad.org/library/article_cdo/aid/1584066/jewish/What-Is-Aliyah.htm.
4. "Pirkei Avot," The JC, accessed January 21, 2020, https://www.thejc.com/judaism/jewish-words/pirkei-avot-1.2573; Naftali Silberber, "Why Is the Tractate Named 'Fathers'?" Chabad.org, accessed October 28, 2024, https://www.chabad.org/library/article_cdo/aid/517534/jewish/Why-is-it-Named-Fathers.htm.
5. "10 Things You Did Not Know About Jerusalem," Mission of Israel to the EU and NATO, May 21, 2018, https://embassies.gov.il/eu/NewsAndEvents/Newsletter/Pages/10-things-you-did-not-know-about-Jerusalem.aspx.
6. "Origins of the Name 'Palestine' and Palestinian Nationalism," Jewish Virtual Library, accessed November 18, 2024, https://www.jewishvirtuallibrary.org/origin-of-quot-palestine-quot
7. "Timeline of Islam," Muslims: Teachers Guide, Frontline, accessed November 18, 2024, https://www.pbs.org/wgbh/pages/frontline/teach/muslims/timeline.html.
8. Mostafa Minawi, "Forgetting the Ottoman Past Has Done the Arabs No Good," *Aljazeera*, August 20, 2023, https://www.aljazeera.com/opinions/2023/8/20/forgetting-the-ottoman-past-has-done-the-arabs-no-good.
9. "Balfour Declaration Letter Written," History.com, updated October 31, 2024, https://www.history.com/this-day-in-history/the-balfour-declaration.
10. "Conference of San Remo," Britannica, accessed November 18, 2024, https://www.britannica.com/event/Conference-of-San-Remo.
11. Alain Gresh, "Yasser Arafat," Britannica, updated November 7, 2024, https://www.britannica.com/biography/Yasser-Arafat.
12. "Palestine Liberation Organization," Britannica, updated October 3, 2024, https://www.britannica.com/topic/Palestine-Liberation-Organization.

13. Deborah Danan, "The Father of Faith-Based Diplomacy," *Jewish Journal*, August 21, 2020, https://jewishjournal.com/israel/320637/the-father-of-faith-based-diplomacy/.

14. Zvika Klein, "Pastor Wants to 'Convert the Church to Love the Torah, Jews,'" *Jerusalem Post*, July 3, 2022, https://www.jpost.com/christianworld/article-711121.

15. Stand for Israel, "The Godfather of the IDF," International Fellowship of Christians and Jews, June 19, 2023, https://www.ifcj.org/news/stand-for-israel-blog/john-henry-patterson-godfather-of-the-idf.

16. "About Us," International March of the Living, accessed November 18, 2024, https://www.motl.org/about/.

17. Reuters, "Massive 'March for Jesus' Rally in Sao Paulo," ABS CBN News, May 31, 2024, https://news.abs-cbn.com/world/2024/5/30/massive-march-for-jesus-rally-in-sao-paulo-532; Evangelical Focus, "Two Million People March for Jesus in São Paulo," Evangelical Focus Europe, June 21, 2017, https://evangelicalfocus.com/life-tech/2660/two-million-people-march-for-jesus-in-sao-paulo.

Chapter 15

1. John Maxwell, "You have to give up to go up," Instagram reel, October 15, 2022, https://www.instagram.com/johncmaxwell/reel/CjvEOaJD2dJ/.

Chapter 16

1. "Kelly Shackelford: Biography," First Liberty, accessed November 18, 2024, https://firstliberty.org/team/kelly-shackelford/.

2. Michael Gryboski, "80 Percent of Protestant Churchgoers Want Pastors to Address Hot Topics: Survey," Christian Post, October 23, 2024, https://www.christianpost.com/news/80-percent-churchgoers-want-pastors-address-current-issues-survey.html.

3. George Barna, "2024 Pre-Election Research—Report #1," Cultural Research Center, Arizona Christian University, October 7, 2024, https://www.arizonachristian.edu/wp-content/uploads/2024/10/CRC-Release-Pre-Election-1-Oct-12-2024-Final.pdf.

4. David Friedman, "Award Presentation at the Israel Allies Foundation's Annual Gala" (speech, Dallas, September 12, 2024).

5. Abby Trivett, "Joni Lamb Receives Tremendous Honor," Charisma News, September 19, 2024, https://charismanews.com/news/joni-lamb-receives-tremendous-honor/.

ABOUT THE AUTHOR

Larry Huch and his wife, Tiz, are the pastors of New Beginnings Church in Bedford, Texas, and hosts of the weekly television broadcast *New Beginnings With Pastors Larry & Tiz Huch*. Across more than forty-five years of ministry the Huchs have planted seven churches in the United States and Australia and written several books individually and together, including *10 Curses That Block the Blessing*; *Releasing Family Blessing*; *No Limits, No Boundaries*; *Free at Last: Breaking Generational Curses*; *The 7 Places Jesus Shed His Blood*; and *Miracles by the Moment*.

The Huchs are dedicated to building bridges of peace, friendship, and unity between Christians and Jews. To that end Larry Huch serves on the board of the Israel Allies Foundation and has received awards from the Knesset Social Welfare Lobby for helping to meet the needs of the Jewish people in Israel.

In February 2020 Pastor Larry received the Israel Allies Lifetime Achievement Award for his thirty years of support for the land and people of Israel. This prestigious honor was awarded by the Knesset Christian Allies Caucus at its thirteenth annual Night to Honor Our Christian Allies, an event to recognize Christian leaders who have been steadfast in their commitment to Israel.

Pastor Larry has been named twice to the prestigious Israel's Top 50 Christian Allies list, in 2020 and 2021. This coveted list includes Christian leaders from around the world who are staunch advocates for Israel.

Most recently, in 2022, Pastor Larry was selected as the first-ever recipient of the John Henry Patterson Guardian of Zion Award. This prestigious award was presented by Keren Hayesod to recognize Pastor Larry's steadfast support for and generosity to Israel and the Jewish people.

The Huchs have three adult children, a daughter-in-law, a son-in-law, and four grandchildren.